WHERE THEY LIVED & WHERE THEY LAY

Homes & Graves of Interesting and Famous People

by Alan McCourt

**FOR
HELEN
(1946 – 2010)**

All profits from this book will be donated to Alzheimer's Research UK

ACKNOWLEDGEMENTS

My thanks to Chris Keeling, of Arc Publishing and Print,
for his much needed support and help.

Also, thanks to Lisa McCourt-Kirk for her help and contributions and to
Brenda Anderson for her assistance and patience.

Contents

First published in the United Kingdom by
Arc Publishing and Print 2021

Copyright © Alan McCourt 2021

ISBN: 978-1-906722-84-5

INTRODUCTION

When compiling a book of this nature, it is almost impossible to establish a definitive finishing point as there are always more houses of notable people to find, more blue plaques to discover and, particularly in the deceased section, new additions almost daily.

In London, homes and houses of famous people often have blue plaques fixed to the outside walls denoting who previously resided at that property.

There are now several organisations that erect blue plaques – the main one in the UK being English Heritage. However, in the provinces, many houses of famous people do not have such attachments.

I am indebted to all the various societies, which are referenced, for all the information that they have amassed over the years.

In the section "Previous Homes of Famous People" no current addresses of living persons have been included unless the information is in the public domain and widely circulated in the press etc.
Also, many notable people have lived in multiple houses so a nominal selection has been shown accordingly. Note: There are not always blue plaques at these locations.

Some properties are open for internal viewing by the public, however, there may be an entrance fee to gain admission.

Whilst some people find viewing cemeteries quite morbid, others find a lot of interest in the many fine examples of architecture displayed, perhaps denoting a grave or, in other cases, a sepulchre or mausoleum to the deceased individual.
In London, there are many excellent examples at Highgate Cemetery (East and West), Kensal Green Cemetery and Brompton Cemetery. On the continent, there are again many interesting cemeteries for example Pere Lachaise in Paris or Vienna Central Cemetery.
Cemeteries can also offer a place of refuge from the busy world that we live in and people often go and sit quietly away from all the noise and bustle of modern life.

In the section "Cemeteries with Famous Graves and Memorials (Worldwide)", only a small number of interments are included as possible visiting suggestions. Obviously, there are very many others that could be added but it is hoped that the traveller will be encouraged to find more during his or her worldly travels.

In California, USA, there are many large cemeteries, with manicured grounds and, usually, a large mausoleum. Many of the film stars, of days gone by, are buried in graves at these sites.

Deceased persons, in the past, have usually been interred and many of the graves are viewable to offer respects. However, in more modern times, cremation has been widely adopted and ashes may have been scattered, sometimes in the crematorium grounds and in other circumstances taken elsewhere. In some instances there are memorial plaques, at the crematoriums, for the departed persons.

It is also interesting to note that there are a number of notable people who have died relatively young in modern terms. For example :-

Buddy Holly (singer –The Crickets) aged 22
Brian Jones (musician – Rolling Stones) aged 27
Jim Morrison (singer – The Doors) aged 27
Jimi Hendrix (singer) aged 27
Marc Bolan (singer T.Rex) aged 29
Karen Carpenter (singer) aged 32
Mama Cass (singer) aged 32
Charlie 'Bird' Parker (Jazz Musician) aged 34
Princess Diana - aged 36
Michael Hutchence (singer – INXS) aged 37
Mario Lanza (singer) aged 38
John Lennon (singer – The Beatles) aged 40
Elvis Presley (singer) aged 42
Tony Hancock (comedian) aged 44
Freddie Mercury (singer) aged 45

Almost all cemeteries are free to visit and some of the larger cemeteries sell guide books to help in finding notable graves.

Happy travelling and researching.

BRIEF NOTES OF SOME INTERESTING PEOPLE

Ove Arup (1895-1988)

Ove Arup was born in Newcastle in 1895 to a Danish father and Norwegian mother.
In 1918 he enrolled for an engineering degree, at the Technical University of Denmark, and specialised in reinforced concrete.
In those early years, Ove Arup was influenced by Le Corbusier and by Walter Gropius, who was the founder of the Bauhaus movement.
Arup worked for various companies and in 1938, formed his own company with his cousin, called Arup and Arup Limited – a firm of engineers and contractors.
The Arup company was kept very busy during WW2.
In 1946, after dissolving Arup and Arup Ltd, he created a team of civil and structural engineers and called it Ove Arup and Partners.
In 1953, Ove Arup received a CBE award.
Following the success of Ove Arup and Partners, a further, additional allied company was formed in 1963, called Arup Associates which is a multi-discipline organisation specialising in engineering and architecture along with other allied building services.
Arup's went on to be consultants on many prestigious buildings including The Sydney Opera House, the Azadi (Liberty) Tower in Tehran, the Crucible Theatre in Sheffield, foundation repairs to York Minster, the London Millennium Bridge and, more recently, the High Speed 2 train project.
Arup was awarded a knighthood in 1971

Henry Boot (1851-1931)

Henry Boot was born a farmer's son just outside Sheffield.
He was apprenticed for 20 years with local building firms, before starting his own business in 1886. The business progressed quickly and was soon working on large public contracts and housing projects.
Henry retired from the business before World War 1 leaving his son, Charles Boot (1874-1945), as managing director.
It was Charles who transformed Henry Boot and Son into one of the most successful construction and housing businesses between the wars.
After World War 1, a Paris office was opened and, in 1920, offices were opened in Athens and Barcelona.
In 1934, Charles Boot embarked on the creation and construction of what would become Pinewood Film Studios at Heatherdean Hall at Iver Heath, Buckinghamshire.
In the 1970's, the company worked on the Mass Transit Railway in Hong Kong and on the Kowloon-Canton Railway.

Peter Brough (1916-1999)

Peter was born on 26th February, 1916, and began his radio career in 1944.
In 1950, he became a radio ventriloquist and introduced his puppet Archie Andrews to his act.

The radio programme Educating Archie featured such future stars as Tony Hancock, Hattie Jacques, Dick Emery, and Benny Hill. The programme had around 15 million listeners and one of the main script writers was Eric Sykes.

A TV series soon followed called Here's Archie, co-starring Irene Handl, but, unfortunately, this showed Peter's limitations as a ventriloquist and the show was soon cancelled.

Peter, eventually, took over running the family menswear business and died on the 3rd June 1999. He was buried in Maldon Cemetery, Essex.

The Archie Andrews doll was sold at auction in 2005 for £34,000

Joe Cocker (1944-2014)

John Robert Cocker (Joe) was born, in Sheffield, on the 20th May 1944 and was a rhythm and blues singer which he performed with spasmodic body movements.

He began his career singing, with his group, in the pubs, clubs and church halls of South Yorkshire, and was known as Vance Arnold and the Avengers.

In 1964, Joe signed a recording contract with Decca but this lapsed in the same year.

He eventually found recording fame in 1968 and, by 1969, was appearing at Woodstock in the USA. This lead to worldwide recognition and, for many years after, he had an acclaimed career.

Unfortunately, his personal lifestyle included alcohol and various drugs, which took its toll with his health. This, subsequently, affected the quality of his singing voice.

He eventually overcame his addictions which resulted in a much improved vocal range.

In 2008, he was invested with an OBE for services to music.

He passed away in December 2014 and is buried in Crawford, Colorado, USA.

Agatha Christie (1890-1976)

Agatha Christie was born into a wealthy upper-middle-class family in Torquay.

She was, initially, an unsuccessful writer and had several rejections.

However, in 1920, a novel was published featuring Hercule Poirot.

In December 1926, Christie had an argument with her husband, as he had fallen in love with another woman. Later the same evening, Christie disappeared from her home and her car was found abandoned the next morning. It was 10 days later that she was located at the Swan Hotel in Harrogate. Opinions remain divided on what caused her disappearance. She divorced her husband in 1928.

Between both World Wars, Christie worked in hospital dispensaries where she acquired her knowledge of poisons which later featured in her novels and short stories.

Christie went on to write 33 novels and 50 short stories featuring Poirot.

Miss Jane Marple began appearing in novels in 1927 and 12 novels and 20 stories were subsequently written featuring her.

Christie also wrote the world's longest running play, The Mousetrap, which premiered in the West End of London in 1952.

She was appointed a CBE in 1956 followed by a DBE in 1971.

Barbara Hepworth (1903-1975)

Barbara Hepworth was born in Wakefield in 1903.
In 1920, she won a scholarship to study at the Leeds School of Art and it was here that she met Henry Moore and began a friendly rivalry.
In 1921, she won a scholarship to attend the Royal College of Art.
Her early work was abstract sculpture and, in 1931, she was the first to sculpt the pierced figures that became a characteristic of her work – later followed by Henry Moore.
In 1949, Hepworth went to live in Trewyn Studios in St Ives until her death in 1975.
The Trewyn Studios are now open to the public as a museum. (Admission charge)
She was appointed a CBE IN 1958 and a DBE in 1965.
The Hepworth (Museum) was also opened in Wakefield in 2011.

Max Miller (1894-1963)

Thomas Henry Sargent was born in Brighton in 1894. He tried an assortment of jobs before signing up for the army at the start of WW1.
Whilst in the army he started a troops concert party.
Following demobilisation, he applied and joined a Brighton beach concert party in 1919, as a comedian.
He married his wife in 1921 and she was an astute business woman. It was her who suggested that he change his name to Max Miller and be billed as the "Cheeky Chappy "
In the 1920's, he was regularly touring in revues and becoming very popular. He, subsequently appeared on the London Palladium, for the first time in 1931.
He appeared several more times at the Palladium in his career and, in 1943, was the highest paid variety artist.
He was known for his colourful suits, plus fours and kipper ties. His act was full off innuendos but he never swore or told a "dirty word" on stage.

William Morris (1834-1896)

William was born in 1834 at Walthamstowe, Essex, into a wealthy middle class family.
After studying Classics at Oxford University, he became friends with Pre-Raphaelites Edward Burne-Jones and Dante Gabriel Rossetti and Neo-Gothic architect Philip Webb.
Morris and Webb went on to design Red House in Kent where Morris began to reside.
He later moved to Red Lion Square, Bloomsbury, London, and formed a decorative arts firm with Burne-Jones, Rossetti and Webb designing tapestries, wallpaper, fabrics, furniture and stained glass windows.
Eventually, Morris moved away from London to Kelmscott Manor Oxfordshire, which he adored.
Morris went on to become one of the most significant cultural figures of Victorian Britain.
He died in 1896 and was buried in the graveyard of St George's Church, Kelmscott.

Charlie Parker (1920-1955)

Charlie "Bird" Parker was born on the 29th August, 1920 and became an extremely talented jazz saxophonist.

When he was 16 years old, he had an accident and he began taking morphine to ease the pain and soon became addicted for the rest of his life.

Musically, he was a pioneer of chord sequences, phrasing and tone .

He lived life to the full but died from pneumonia following years of drug addiction, mental illness and attempted suicides. At his death, in 1955, he was just 34 years old and was buried in Lincoln Cemetery, Missouri.

Al Read (1909-1987)

Al Read was born in Broughton, Salford in 1909.

He worked, for a while, in his father's business as a meat processor and later became known on the club circuit with his observational humour – particularly about northern working class society.

He made his debut with the BBC in 1950 and appeared on Workers Playtime and Variety Bandbox. He later had his own show, the Al Read Show, which became one of the most popular radio comedy shows in the UK.

In 1954 he appeared on the bill of the Royal Variety Performance at the London Palladium.

He continued with his radio shows until 1976 after which he just faded away and lived in semi-retirement.

Al died in September 1987 in Northallerton, Yorkshire. No details of the interment available.

P.L Travers (1899-1996)

Pamela Lyndon Travers was an author, particularly known for her book, Mary Poppins. She was born Helen Lyndon Goff in 1899 in Australia.

Her first work was published whilst she was a teenager and, at the age of 25 years old, she emigrated to England and adopted the pen name of P.L. Travers.

She wrote the first Mary Poppins short story in 1926 followed by seven sequels – the last being in 1988 when Travers was 89.

She had a very dysfunctional lifestyle and never married.

She was appointed an OBE in 1977 and passed away in 1996 aged 96.

She is buried in St Mary's Churchyard, Twickenham, London

Rudolf Valentino (1895-1926)

Valentino was born in Italy to an Italian father and French mother. He was rejected from military service so, in 1922, he went to Paris but failed to secure work there.

The following year, he made his way to New York where he had several menial jobs including a dancer.

He then went to Hollywood but, initially, only landed 'bit' parts in films. However, in 1921, he was cast in a lead roll and the film became a box-office hit. This was followed by several other major films which, eventually, made him a romantic hero.

He was married several times - mainly unsuccessfully. In 1926, whilst on a promotional tour, he become ill with appendicitis which developed into peritonitis.

He died in 1926 aged 31. Although he had found great success in America he never obtained naturalisation papers so retained his Italian citizenship.

PREVIOUS HOMES OF FAMOUS PEOPLE (UK)

ADAM, Robert (1728-1792) Architect
1-3 Robert Street, Adelphi, London WC2
11 Albemarle Street, London
20 St James's Square, London

ARKWRIGHT, Richard (1732-1792) Industrialist and Inventor
8 Adam Street, London WC

ARNE, Thomas (1710-1778) Composer
31 King Street, Covent Garden, London
215 Kings Road, Chelsea, London

ARUP, Ove (1895-1988) Structural Engineer
6 Fitzroy Park, Highgate, London
28 Willifield Way, Barnet, London

ASHLEY, Laura (1925-1985) Fashion
83 Cambridge Street, Pimlico, London SW1V 4PS
35 Maengwyn Street, Machynlleth, Powys

ASHTON, Frederick (1904-1988) Choreographer
8 Marlborough Street, Chelsea

ASQUITH, Herbert Henry (1852-1928) Politician
20 Cavendish Square, London W1
12 Keats Grove, Hampstead, London
Croft House, Church Street, Morley, Yorkshire

ASTOR, Nancy (1879-1964) first women to sit in Parliament
4 St James' Square, London

ATTLEE, Richard Clement (1883-1967) British Prime Minister
17 Monkmans Avenue, Woodford Green, Redbridge
18 Portinscale Road, Putney, London
Cherry Cottage, Green Lane, Great Missenden

BABBAGE, Charles (1791-1871) Mathematician
44 Crosby Row, Newington, London

BACALL, Lauren (1924-2014) Actress
Claridge's Hotel, Brook Street, Mayfair, London

BACON, Francis (1909-1992) Artist
7 Reece Mews, Kensington, London

BADEN-POWELL, Robert (1857-1941) Chief Scout
9 Hyde Park Gate, London SW7
11 Stanhope Terrace, Paddington, London

BADER, Douglas (1910-1982) RAF fighter pilot
5 Petersham Mews, Kensington, London

BAIRD, John Logie (1888-1946) Television Pioneer
3 Crescent Wood Road, Sydenham, London SE26
21 Linton Crescent, Hastings, Sussex
57 Ellerby Street, Fulham, London
22 Frith Street, Soho, London

BALDWIN, Stanley (1867-1947) British Prime Minister
93 Eaton Square, London SW1
Lower Park House, Bewdley
27 Queens Gate, London

BARBIROLLI, John (1899-1970) Classical Conductor
Born: Bloomsbury Park Hotel,
Southampton Row, London

BARNARDO, Thomas (1845-1905) Founder of homes for
children. 32 Bow Road, Tower Hamlets, London

BARRIE, J.M (1860-1937) Novelist
100 Bayswater Road, London W2 3HJ
1-3 Robert Street, Charring Cross, London WC2N 6BN
133 Gloucester Road, Kensington, London
Bernard Street (corner of Grenville Street) now demolished

BARRY, Charles (1795-1860) Architect (Houses of Parliament)
29 Clapham Common North Side

BARTOK, Bela (1881-1945) Classical Composer
7 Sydney Place, South Kensington, London (stayed here frequently)

BAZALGETTE, Joseph William (1819-1891) Civil Engineer
17 Hamilton Terrace, St John's Wood, London

BEATON, Cecil (1904-1980) Fashion Designer
8 Pelham Place, Kensington, London
36 Chesham Place, Belgravia, London

BEAUFORT, Francis (1774-1857) Beaufort Wind Scale
52 Manchester Street, Marylebone, London

BECK, Harry (1902-1974) Designer of London Underground map
18 Wesley Road, Leyton, London

BEE GEES, Popular Singing Group
51 Keppel Road, Chorlton cum Hardy, Manchester

BEECHAM, Thomas (1879-1961) Classical Conductor
31 Grove End Road, St John's Wood, London

BELLOC, Hilaire (1870-1953) Poet, Essayist
104 Cheyne Walk, London

BEN-GURION, David (1886-1973) first Prime Minister of Israel
75 Warrington Crescent, Maida Vale, London

BENN, Tony (1925-2014) Politician
12 Holland Park Avenue, Notting Hill Gate, London W11 3QU

BENNETT, Alan (1934-) Satirist, Author
23 Gloucester Crescent, Camden, London

BENNETT, William Sterndale (1816-1875) Composer
38 Queensborough Terrace, Bayswater, London

BERLIOZ, Hector (1803-1869) Classical Composer
58 Queen Anne Street, London (stayed here in 1851)

BETJEMEN, John (1906 -1984) Poet
31 Highgate West Hill, London

BEVAN, Aneurin (1897-1960) politician
23 Cliveden Place, Chelsea, London

BEVIN, Ernest (1881-1951) Trade Union Leader
34 South Moulton Street, London
130 The Vale, Cricklewood, London

BLACK, Cilla (1943-2015) Singer
380 Scotland Road, Liverpool

BLAIR, Tony (1953-) Politician and Prime Minister
10 Stavordale Road, Highbury, London
1 Richmond Crescent, Islington, London
Connaught Square, London

BLANCHFLOWER, Danny (1926-1993) Footballer
49 Grace Avenue, Belfast, N.Ireland

BLIGH, William (1754-1817) Commander of the "Bounty"
100 Lambeth Road, London

BLISS, Arthur (1891-1975) Classical Composer
East Heath Lodge, 1 East Heath Road, Hampstead, London
8 The Lane, Marlborough Place, St John's Wood, London

BLYTON, Enid (1897-1968) Children's Writer
207 Hook Road, Chessington, Kingston upon Thames
Beaufort Mansions, Beaufort Street, Chelsea, London
82 Shortlands Road, Bromley

BOLAN, Marc (1947-1977) Singer "T Rex"
25 Stoke Newington Common, Hackney, London
25 Holmead Road, Chelsea, London
Somerset House, 79/81 Lexham Gardens, London

BOLIVAR, Simon (1783-1830) Liberator of Latin America
4 Duke Street, London (lodged here)

BOSWELL, James (1740-1795) Biographer
122 Great Portland Street, London

BOULT, Adrian (1889-1983) Classical Conductor
Flat 78, Marlborough Mansions, Cannon Hill, West Hampstead, London
68 Compayne Gardens, West Hampstead, London

BOWIE, David (1947-2016) Singer
Born: 40 Stansfield Road, Brixton, London
9 Denmark Street, London

BRITTAIN, Vera (1893-1970) Author, Nurse
58 Doughty Street, Holborn, London

BRITTEN, Benjamin (1913-1976) Classical Composer
173 Cromwell Road, Earls Court, London
2 West Cottages, Camden, London
The Red House, Golf Lane, Aldeburgh, Suffolk

BROWN, Ford Maddox (1821-1893) Artist
37 Fitzroy Square, London
17 Newman Street, Fitzrovia, London
56 Fortress Road, Kentish Town, London

BROWN, John (1816-1896) Steel Industrialist
Endcliffe Hall, Ranmoor, Sheffield

BROWN, Lancelot "Capability" (1716-1783) landscape architect
Wilderness House, Moat Lane, Hampton Court, London

BROWNING, Elizabeth Barrett (1806-1861) Poet
99 Gloucester Place, London

BRUMMELL, Beau (1778-1840) Leader of Fashion
4 Chesterfield Street, Mayfair, London

BRUNEL, Marc Isambard (1769-1849) Civil Engineer
98 Cheyne Walk, London

BRUNEL, Isambard Kingdom (1806-1859) Civil Engineer
98 Cheyne Walk, London

BURNE-JONES, Edward (1833-1898) Artist
17 Red Lion Square, Holborn, London
41 Kensington Square, Kensington, London

BURTON, Richard (1925-1984) Actor
6 Lyndhurst Road, Hampstead, London

CADBURY, George (1839-1922) Chocolate Manufacturer
32 George Road, Birmingham,
Northfield Manor House, Bristol Road South, Birmingham

CADBURY, Richard (1835-1899) Chocolate Manufacturer
17 Wheeley's Road, Birmingham

CAINE, Michael (1933-) Actor
Grange Croft, Church Street, Dronfield, Sheffield
Mill House, Mill Lane, Windsor
Keston Lodge, Downs Lane, Leatherhead, Surrey

CANAL, Antonio (CANALETTO) (1697-1768) Painter
41 Beak Street, London

CARTE, Richard D'Oyle (1844-1901) Opera Impresario
2 Dartmouth Park Road, Kentish Town, London
President Hotel (house on this site) Guilford Street,
London

CARTER, Henry Vandyke (1831-1897) Surgeon, Anatomical Artist
2 Belgrave Crescent, Scarborough

CARTER, Howard (1874-1939) Egyptologist
19 Collingham Gardens, Earls Court, London
49 Albert Court, Prince Consort Road, Kensington, London

CARTLAND, Barbara (1901-2000) Author
Camfield Place, Hatfield, Hertfordshire

CHAMBERLAIN, Neville (1869-1940) British Prime Minister
37 Eaton Square, London
Highfield Park, Church Lane, Hook, Hampshire

CHANDLER, Raymond (1888-1959) Author
110 Auckland Road, Upper Norwood, London

CHAPLIN, Charlie (1889-1977) Comedy Film Actor
Born: East Street, Walworth, London
287 Kennington Lane, Kennington, London
15 Glenshaw Mansions, Brixton Road, London
39 Methley Street, Walworth, London

CHESTERTON, Gilbert Keith (1874-1936) Poet, Novelist
11 Warwick Gardens, Kensington, London
32 Sheffield Terrace, Kensington, London

CHEVALIER, Albert (1861-1923) Music Hall Comedian
17 St Ann's Villas, Holland Park, London (born here)

CHIPPENDALE, Thomas (1718-1779) Cabinet Maker
61 St Martin's Lane, London

CHOPIN, Frederic (1810-1849) Composer
4 St James' Place, London

CHRISTIE, Agatha (1890-1976) Novelist
22 Cresswell Place, London
58 Sheffield Terrace, Kensington, London
5 Northwick Terrace, St John's Wood, London

CHURCHILL, Winston (1874-1965) British Prime Minister
28 Hyde Park Gate, Kensington Gore, London
34 Ecclestone Square, Belgravia, London

CLARK, Arthur C. (1917-2008) Fiction Writer
Blenheim Road, Minehead, Somerset

CLEESE, John (1939-) Actor, screenwriter, producer
The Mount, Esher, Surrey

CLEMENS, Samuel Langhorne (1835-1910) Author Mark Twain
23 Tedworth Square, Chelsea, London

CLIFF, Clarice (1899-1972) Pottery Designer
Born: Fuller Street, Tunstall, Stoke on Trent
Lived: Chetwynd House, Clayton, Stoke

CLIVE of India (1725-1774) Soldier and Administrator
45 Berkley square, London

COATES, Eric (1886-1957) Classical composer
Chiltern Court, Baker Street, London. 7 Willifield Way, London

14

COCKER, Joe (1944-2014) Rock/ blues Musician
38 Tasker Road, Crookes, Sheffield

COGAN, Alma (1932-1966) Singer
44 Stafford Court, Kensington High Street, London

CONAN DOYLE, Arthur (1859-1930) Author
12 Tennison Road, South Norwood, London
2 Upper Wimpole Street, Marylebone, London

CONNERY, Sean (1930-2020) Actor
Centre Avenue, Acton Park, London

CONRAD, Joseph (1857-1924) Novelist
17 Gillingham Street, London
Pent Farm, Postling, Hythe, Kent

CONSTABLE, John (1776-1837) Artist
40 Well Walk, Hampstead, London
Mill House, Dedham, Suffolk
49 Frith Street, Soho, London

CONWAY, Russ (1925-2000) Pianist. Musician
2 Dean Lane, Southville, Bristol

COOK, James (Captain) (1728-1779) Circumnavigator and Explorer
88 Mile End Road, London (lived in a house on this site)
22 Clapham Common North Side, Clapham, London

COOK, Peter (1937-1995) Satirist
17 Church Row, Hampstead, London
Bythom, Bronshill Road, Torquay, Devon

COOKE, Alastair (1908-2004) Broadcaster
7 Isaac Street, Salford, Manchester

COOKSON, Catherine (1906-1998) Author
The Hurst, 114 Hoads Wood Road, Hastings

COOPER, Henry (1934-2011) Boxer
120 Farmstead Road, Catford, London
15 Barley House, Hildenbrook Farm, Hildenborough

COOPER, Jilly (1937-) Author
Ilkley Hall, Ilkley, Yorkshire

COOPER, Tommy (1921-1984) Comedian/magician
19 Llwyn Onn Street, Caerphilly. 51 Barrowgate Road, Chiswick,
London W4 4QT. 13 Canfield Gardens, London NW6

COTTON, Henry (1907-1987) Golfer
47 Crystal Palace Road, Dulwich, London

COWARD, Noel (1899-1973) Actor, Playwright
131 Waldegrave Road, Teddington, London
17 Gerald Road, Belgravia, London
Goldenhurst, Adlington, Kent

CRADDOCK, Fanny (1909-1994) T.V. Cook
Fairwood Court, Fairlop Road, London E11

CRAPPER, Thomas (1837-1910) Plumber and Engineer
12 Thornsett Road, Bromley

CRIPPEN, Dr Hawley Harvey (1862-1910) Homeopathic Physician
39 Hilldrop Crescent, Camden Road, Holloway, London
34-37 Store Street, Bloomsbury, London

CRIPPS, Stafford (1889-1952) Statesman
32 Elm Park Gardens, London
Oakridge, Frith Hill, Stroud

CROMPTON, Richmal (1890-1969) Author
The Glebe, Oakley Road, Bromley Common

CUBITT, Thomas (1788-1855) Master Builder
3 Lyall Street, Belgravia, London

CUSHING, Peter (1913-1994) Actor
32 St James' Road, Purley, London

DANDO, Jill (1961-1999) Journalist and T.V.Presenter
29 Gowan Avenue, Fulham, London

DARWIN, Charles (1809-1882) Naturalist
(site of 110) 12 Gower Street, London

DAVIS, Ray (1944-) Singer
87 Fortis Green, Muswell Hill, London N2 9HU

DAVIS, Joe (1901-1978) Snooker player
80 Welbeck Street, Whitwell, Derbyshire

DAVIS, Mandy Rice (1944-2014) Model
1 Bryanston Mews, Paddington, London

DAWSON, Les (1931-1993) Comedian
The Bumbles, 19 Islay Road, Lytham St Anne's

DEFOE, Daniel (1661-1731) Novelist
95 Stoke Newington Church Street, London

DE HAVILLAND, Geoffrey (1882-1965) Aircraft Designer
32 Baron's Court Road, Kensington, London

DE LA MARE, Walter (1873-1956) Poet
South End House, Montpelier Row, Twickenham, London

DELANEY, Shelagh (1938-2011) Author
77 Duchy Road, Salford, Manchester

DELIUS, Frederick (1862-1934) Classical Composer
44 Belsize Park Gardens, London

DICKENS, Charles (1812-1870) Novelist
48 Doughty Street, London
16 Bayham Street, Camden, London
1 Devonshire Terrace, Marylebone, London

DIMBLEBY, Richard (1913-1965) broadcaster
20 Cedar Court, Sheen Lane, East Sheen

DISRAELI, Benjamin (1804-1881) Statesman
Lived 22 Theobalds Road, London
Died 19 Curzon Street, London
6 Bloomsbury Square, Bloomsbury, London

DIXON, Reginald (1904-1985) Theatre Organist
3 Orchard Avenue, Poulton le Fylde

DODD, Ken (1927-2018) Comedian
70-76 Thomas Lane, Liverpool 14

DONAT, Robert (1905-1958) Actor
8 Meadway, Hampstead Garden Suburb, London
8 The Grove, Highgate, London

DE VALOIS, Ninette (1898-2001) Founder of the Royal Ballet
14 The Terrace, Barnes, London

DU PRE, Jaqueline (1945-1987) Cellist
6A Pilgrim Lane, Hampstead, London
27 Upper Montagu Street, London
14 The Bridle Road, Purley, Surrey

ELIN, Gus (1862-1940) Music Hall Comedian
3 Thurleigh Avenue, Balham, London SW12
Edith Villa, 3 Thurleigh Avenue, London

ELGAR, Edward (1857-1934) Classical Composer
51 Avonmore Road, Kensington, London W14
The Firs, Crown East Lane, Lower Broadheath, Worcestershire
Craeg Lea, Wells Road, Malvern

ELIOT, George (Mary Ann Evans) (1819-1880) Novelist
4 Cheyne Walk, London
Holly Lodge, 31 Wimbledon Park Road, London SW18

ELIOT, T.S. (1888-1965) Poet
3 Kensington Court Gardens, Kensingon, London W8

ENGLISH, Arthur (1919-1995) Comedian, Actor
22 Lysons Road, Aldershot

ENTWISLE, John (1944-2003) Band member of "The Who"
Quarwood House, Stow on the Wold, Gloucestershire

EPSTEIN, Brian (1934-1967) The Beatles Manager
24 Chapel Street, Belgravia, London
4 Rodney Street, Liverpool

EPSTEIN, Jacob (1880-1959) Sculptor
18 Hyde Park Gate, London

EVANS, Edith (1888-1976) Actress
109 Ebury Street, Victoria, London SW1

EVERETT, Kenny (Maurice Cole) (1944-1995)
Radio and T.V. Personality
14 Hereford Road, Seaforth, Liverpool
91 Lexham Gardens, London

FARADAY, Michael (1791-1867) Scientist
48 Blandford Street, Marylebone, London

FERRIER, Kathleen (1912-1953) Contralto
97 Frognal Walk, Hampstead, London NW3
40 Hamilton Terrace, St John's Wood, London

FIELDING, Henry (1707-1754) Novelist
Milbourne House, Barnes Green, London SW13

FIELDS, Gracie (1898-1979) Singer and Entertainer
9 Molesworth Street Rochdale
72A Upper Street, Islington, London
La Canzone del Mare, Capri
20 Frognal Way, Hampstead, London

FIRTH, Mark (1819-1880) Steel Industrialist
Oakbrook, Ranmoor, Sheffield

FLANAGAN, Bud (1896-1968) Comedian
12 Hanbury Street, London E1 (born here)
503 Raleigh House, Dolphin Square, London
Riverside, Riversdale, Bourne End

FLANDERS, Michael (1922-1975) Performer of comic songs
1 Scarsdale Villas, Kensington, London

FLEMING, Alexander (1881-1955) Discoverer of Penicillin
20a Danvers Street, London SW3

FLEMING, Ian (1908-1964) Novelist
22 Ebury Street, Victoria, London SW1
119 Cheyne Walk, Chelsea, London
16 Victoria Square, Victoria, London

FONTEYN, Margot (1919-1991) Prima Ballerina
118 Long Acre, London, WC2E 9PA
49 London Road, Ryegate, Surrey
19 Pelham Crescent, Kensington, London

FORESTER, C.S. (1899-1966) Novelist
58 Underhill Road, Dulwich, London SE22

FORMBY, George (1904-1961) Entertainer
Beryldene, 199 Inner Promenade, Fairhaven,
Lytham St. Annes
Beryldene, Mains Lane, Poulton-le-Fylde

FORSYTH, Bruce (1928-2017) Comedian/ entertainer
Straidarran, Wentworth Drive, Virginia Water, Surrey GU25 4NY
95 Victoria Road, Edmonton, London
The Paddocks, 22 Totteridge Common, Totteridge, London

FRANKLIN, Benjamin (1706-1790) American Statesman and Scientist
36 Craven Street, London WC2
Ormathwaite Hall, Keswick, Cumbria

FREUD, Sigmund (1856-1939) Founder of Psychoanalysis
20 Maresfield Gardens, London NW3
39 Elsworthy Road, Primrose Hill, London

FURY, Billy (1940-1983) Singer
Haliburton Street, Liverpool
1 Cavendish Avenue, St John's Wood, London

GAINSBOROUGH, Thomas (1727-1788) Painter
Born: 46 Gainsborough Street, Sudbury, Suffolk
82 Pall Mall, London SW1

GAITSKELL, Hugh (1906-1963) Statesman
18 Frognal Gardens, Hampstead, London NW3
3 Airlie Gardens, Kensington, London

GANDHI, Mahatma (1869-1948) Philosopher
20 Baron's Court Road, London W14 (lived here as a student)

GARDNER, Ava (1922-1990) Actress
34 Ennismore Gardens, Knightsbridge, London

GARLAND, Judy (1922-1969) Singer and Entertainer
4 Cadogan Lane, Chelsea, London (site now re-developed)

GARRICK, David (1717-1779) Actor
Garrick's Villa, Hampton Court Road, Richmond upon Thames

GIBB, Barry (1946-) Singer, Bee Gees
65 Eaton Square, Belgravia, London

GIBB, Robin (1949-2012) Singer, Bee Gees
The Prebendal, Thame, Oxford
50 St Catherine's Drive, Douglas, Isle of Man

GIBSON, Guy (1918-1944) Pilot Dambusters Raid
32 Aberdeen Place, St John's Wood, London

GILBERT, W.S. (1836-1911) Gilbert and Sullivan
39 Harrington Gardens, Kensington, London SW7
90 Eaton Square, Belgravia, London

GLADSTONE, William Ewart (1809-1898) Statesman
11 Carlton House Terrace, London SW1
73 Harley Street, London

GOLDFINGER, Erno (1902-1987) Architect
1-3 Willow Road, Hampstead, London

GOUNOD, Charles (1818-1893) Classical Composer
15 Morden Road, Blackheath, London SE3

GRACE, W.G. (1848-1915) Cricketer
"Fairmount" Mottingham Lane, London SE9
15 Victoria Square, Clifton, Avon

GRAHAME, Kenneth (1859-1932) Novelist
16 Phillimore Place, Holland Park, London W8

GRAINGER, Percy (1882-1961) Australian Composer
31A King's Road, Chelsea, London SW3

GRANGER, Stewart (1913-1993) Film Actor
East Cliff, Cottage Hotel, Grove Road, Bournemouth
Coleherne Court, Flat 6, Old Brompton Road, London
37 Belgrave Square, Belgravia, London

GRAY, Henry (1827-1861) Surgeon, Author Gray's Anatomy
8 Wilton Street, London

GREENE, Graham (1904-1991) Author
14 Clapham Common North Side

GRENFELL, Joyce (1910-1979) Entertainer and writer
34 Elm Park Gardens, Chelsea, London

GRESLEY, Nigel (1876-1941) Railway Engineer
Old Rectory, Ashby Road, Netherseal, Derbyshire

GRIMALDI, Joseph (1778-1837) Clown
56 Exmouth Market, Islington, London EC1

GIELGUD, John (1904-2000) Actor
16 Cowley Street, London SW1

GRIEG, Edvard (1843-1907) Composer
47 Clapham Common North Side

GUINNESS, Alec (1914-2000) Actor
Kettlebrook Meadows, Steep Marsh, Petersfield, Hampshire
The Brook, Stamford Brook Road, Chiswick, London
7 St Peter's Square, Hammersmith, London

HALL, Henry (1898-1989) Band Leader
38 Harman Drive, Cricklewood, London NW2
8 Randolph Mews, Maida Vale, London

HALL, Radclyffe (1880-1943) Author and Poet
37 Holland Street, Kensington, London

HALLE, Charles (1819-1895) Founder of Halle Orchestra
Addison Terrace, Daisy Bank Road, Victoria Park, Manchester

HANCOCK, Tony (1924-1968) Comedy Actor
Born: 41 Southam Road, Hall Green, Birmingham
20 Queen's Gate Place, Kensington, London
10 Greys Close, Hampstead, London

HANDEL, George Frederick (1685-1759) Classical Composer
25 Brook Street, Mayfair, London W1

HANDLEY, Tommy (1892-1949) Radio Comedian
34 Craven Road, Paddington, London W2
29 Cleveland Gardens, Paddington, London

HANDLEY PAGE, Frederick (1885-1962) Aircraft designer and
manufacturer. 18 Grosvenor Square, Mayfair, London

HANSOM, Joseph Aloysius (1803-1882) Architect and Inventor of
Hansom Cab. 27 Sumner Place, Kensington, London SW7

HARDY, Thomas (1840-1928) Poet and Novelist
172 Trinity Road, Tooting, London SW17
9 Wynnstay Gardens, Kensington, London

HARRISON, George (1943-2001) Musician "The Beatles"
12 Arnold Grove, Liverpool
25 Upton Green, Speke, Liverpool
Kinfaus, Claremont Drive, Esher, London
Friar Park, Henley on Thames, London

HARRISON, John (1693-1776) Inventor of Marine Chronometer
Summit House, 12 Red Lion Square, London WC1 (house on this site)

HARRISON, Rex (1908-1990) Actor
75 Eaton Square, Belgravia, London

HAWTRY, Charles (1914-1988) Comedy Actor ("Carry On" films)
117 Middle Street, Deal

HAY, Will (1888-1949) Comic Actor and Astronomer
45 The Chase, Norbury, London SW16
The White lodge, Great North Way, Hendon, London
Flat 2, 16 Chelsea Embankment, Chelsea, London

HAYES, Tubby (1935- 1973) Jazz musician
34 Kenwyn Road, Wimbledon, London SW20

HAYNES, Arthur (1914-1966) Comedian
74 Gunnersbury Avenue, Ealing Common, London

HEATH, Edward (1916-2005) Prime Minister
1 Holmwood Villas, Albion Road, Broadstairs, Kent
Arundells, 59 Cathedral Close, Salisbury
F2 Albany, Mayfair, London

HEATH ROBINSON, W. (1872-1944) Illustrator and Comic Artist
75 Moss Lane, Pinner, London

HENDRIX, Jimmy (1942-1970) Guitarist and Songwriter
23 Brook Street, Mayfair, London W1
34 Montagu Square, Marylebone, London

HENSON, Jim (1936-1990) Creator of the Mupppets
50 Downshire Hill, Hampstead, London

HEPWORTH, Barbara (1903-1975) Sculptor, Artist
Trewyn Studios, St Ives, Cornwall

HERSCHEL, William (1738-1822) Astronomer
19 King Street, Bath

HESS, Myra (1890-1965) Pianist
48 Wildwood Road, Hampstead, London

HILL, Benny (1924-1992) Comedian
Roof Flat, 1 Queen's Gate, Kensington, London
Flat 7, Fairwater House, 34 Twickenham Road,
Teddington, London

HILL, Graham (1929-1975) Racing driver
32 Parkside, Mill Hill, London

HILL, Rowland (1795-1879) Postal reformer
1 Orme Square, Bayswater, London

HITCHCOCK, Alfred (1899-1980) Film Director
153 Cromwell Road, Earls Court, London SW5

HOBBS, Jack (1882-1963) Cricketer
17 Englewood Road, London SW12

HOGARTH, William (1697-1764) Artist
Hogarth Lane, Chiswick, London

HOLLOWAY, Stanley (1890-1982) Actor and Humourist
25 Albany Road, Newham, London
112 Northwick Park Avenue, Kenton, London
Pyefleet, Tamarisk Way, East Preston, West Sussex

HOLMAN HUNT, William (1827-1910) Artist
18 Melbury Road, Holland Park, London

HOLST, Gustav (1874-1934) Composer
4 Clarence Road, Cheltenham

HORNBY, Frank (1863-1936) Toy Manufacturer
The Hollies, Station Road, Maghull, Liverpool

HOUDINI, Harry (1874-1926) Magician
10 Keppel Street, Bloomsbury, London
(now demolished)

HOWERD, Frankie (1917-1992) Comedian
27 Edwardes Square, Kensington, London
46 Brook Street, Mayfair, London

HOYLE, Fred (1915-2001) Astronomer
Keighley Road, Bingley, Yorkshire

HUNTER, John (1728-1793) Surgeon
31 Golden Square, London

IRVING, Henry (1838-1905) Actor
15A Grafton Street, Mayfair, London

JACQUES, Hattie (1922-1980) Comedy Actress
67 Eardley Crescent, Earls Court, London
13 Thurloe Place, Kensington, London

JAGGER, Charles Sargeant (1885-1934) Sculptor
67 Albert Bridge Road, Battersea, London

JAGGER, Mick (1943-) Singer "Rolling Stones"
Downe House, Richmond Hill, London
48 Cheyne Walk, Chelsea, London
39 Denver Road, Dartford, Kent

JAMES, Sid (1913-1976) Comedy Actor
35 Gunnersbury Avenue, Ealing Common, London
31 Compayne Gardens, Hampstead, London
Delavford Park, Iver, Buckinghamshire

JEROME, Jerome K. (1859-1927)
Author of "Three Men in a Boat"
91-104 Chelsea Gardens,
Chelsea Bridge Road, London SW1
32 Tavistock Place, Bloomsbury, London

JOHN, Elton (Reginald Kenneth Dwight) (1947-) Singer
Born: 55 Pinner Hill Road, Pinner, London
Potter Street, Northwood Hills, Middlesex

JOHNSON, Amy (1903-1941) Aviator
Vernon Court, Hendon Way, London NW2

JOHNSON, Samuel (1709-1784) Author
Market Square, Lichfield
17 Gough Square, London

JONES, Brian (1942-1969) Musician with "Rolling Stones"
Cotchford Farm, Hartfield, East Sussex
335 Hatherley Road, Cheltenham
102 Edith Grove, Chelsea, London

JONES, Tom (1940-) Singer
Socknersh Manor, Etchingham, East Sussex

JOYCE, James (1882-1941) Author
28 Campden Grove, Kensington, London W8
41 Brighton Square, Dublin, Ireland

KARLOFF, Boris (1887-1969) Actor
36 Forest Hill Road, East Dulwich, London (born here)
Roundabout Cottage, Tunbridge Lane, Bramshott, Hampshire

KEATS, John (1795-1821) Poet
"Keats House", Keats Grove, Hampstead, London NW3
25 Great College Street, Westminster, London
26 Piazza de Spagna, Rome

KEELER, Christine (1942-2017) Model
1 Bryanston Mews, Paddington, London W1H 2BW

KELVIN, Lord (1824-1907) Physicist and Inventor
15 Eaton Place, London SW1

KING, Hetty (1883-1972) Music Hall Male Impersonator
17 Palmerston Road, Wimbledon, London

KIPLING, Rudyard (1865-1936) Poet and Story Writer
43 Villiers Street, London WC2
The Elms, The Green, Rottingdean, West Sussex

KITCHENER of Khartoum, Field Marshall (1850-1916)
2 Carlton Gardens, London SW1
17 Belgrave Square, Belgravia, London

KORDA, Alexander (1893-1956) Film Producer
21/22 Grosvenor Street, London W1

KNIGHT, Laura (1877-1970) Artist
16 Langford Place, St John's Wood, London

KRAY, Ronald and Reggie (1933-1995) Criminals
178 Vallance Road, Bethnal Green, London

KWOUK, Burt (1930-2016) Actor
6 Agamemnon Road, West Hampstead, London

LAMBERT, Constant (1905-1951) Composer
197 Albany Street, Regents Park, London

LANGTRY, Lillie (1853-1929) Actress
Cadogan Hotel, 22 Pont Street, London SW1

LAUDER, Harry (1870-1950) Music Hall Artist
46 Longley Road, Tooting, London SW17
Lauder Hal, Colinhill Road, Strathaven, Lanarkshire

LAUGHTON, Charles (1899-1962) Actor
15 Percy Street,Fitzrovia, London W1

LAUREL, Stan (1890-1965) Comedy Film Actor
3 Argyle Street, Ulverston
8 Dockwray Square, North Shields, Newcastle

LAWRENCE, D.H. (1885-1930) Author
8a Victoria Street, Eastwood, Nottinghamshire
Breach House, 28 Garden Road, Eastwood, Nottinghamshire
32 Well Walk, Hampstead, London
1 Byron Villas, Hampstead, London

LAWRENCE, T.E. (1888-1935) "Lawrence of Arabia"
14 Barton Street, London SW1
2 Polstead Road, Oxford

LEAR, Edward (1812-1888) Artist and Writer
30 Seymour Street, London W1
15 Stratford Place, Mayfair, London

LE CARRE, John (1931-2020) Author
9 Gainsborough Garden, Hampstead, London

LEIGH, Vivien (1913-1967) Actress
54 Eaton Square, London SW1
Tickerage Mill, Uckfield, East Sussex

LEIGHTON, Frederick (1830-1896) Painter
Leighton House, 12 Holland Park Road, London W14
2 Orme Square, Bayswater, London

LENNON, John (1940-1980) Musician "The Beatles"
251 Menlove Avenue, Woolton, Liverpool
94 Baker Street, London
Kenwood, St George's Estate, Weybridge, Surrey
Dakota Building, West 72nd Street, New York

LENIN, Vladimir Ilyich (1870-1936)
Founder of USSR
36 Tavistock Place, Bloomsbury, London
16 Percy Circus, Bloomsbury, London

LENO, Dan (1860-1904) Music Hall Comedian
56 Akerman Road, London SW9

LEVER, William Hesketh (1851-1925) Soap Maker and Philanthropist
Inverforth House, North End Way, London NW3

LEYBOURNE, George (1842-1884) Music Hall Comedian ("Champagne Charlie")
136 Englefield Road, Islington, London N1

LISTER, Anne (1791-1840) Landowner, diarist (Gentleman Jack)
Shibden Hall, Halifax

LISTER, Joseph (1827-1912) Surgeon
12 Park Crescent, London W1
9 Charlotte Square, Edinburgh

LITTLE TICH (Harry Relph) (1867-1928) Music Hall Comedian
93 Shirehill Park, Brent Cross, London

LLOYD GEORGE, David (1863-1945) British Prime Minister
3 Routh Road, Wandsworth Common, London SW18
10 Cheyne Walk, Chelsea, London

LLOYD, Marie (1870-1922) Music Hall Artist
55 Graham Road, Hackney, London E8
37 Woodstock Road, Golders Green, London

LOWE, Arthur (1915-1982) Actor
Born : Kinder Road, Hayfield
2 Maida Avenue, Maida Vale, London

LOWRIE, Laurence Stephen (1887-1976) Artist
The Elms, Stalybridge, Mottram, Manchester

LUCAN, Arthur (1885-1954) "Entertainer "Old Mother Riley"
11 Forty Lane, Wembley, London
46 Randall Avenue, Dollis Hill, London
Old Mother Riley's Cottage, Church Lane, Sibsey, Lincs

LUCAN, Lord (1934-?) British Peer (presumed dead)
72a Elizabeth Street, London
19 Bentinck Street, Marylebone, London
46 Lower Belgrave Street, Belgravia, London

LUMLEY, Joanna (1946-) Actress
24 Trebovir Road, Earls Court, London SW5 9NJ

LUTYENS, Edwin, Landseer (1869-1944) Architect
13 Mansfield Street, Marylebone, London

LYONS, Joseph (1847-1917) Lyons Tea Shops
11A Palace Mansions, Hammersmith Road, London

MACDONALD, Ramsey (1866-1937) British Prime Minister
9 Howitt Road, London NW3
3 Lincoln's Inn Fields, Holborn, London
Upper Frognal Lodge, Frognal, Hampstead, London

MARCONI, Guglielmo (1874-1937)
Pioneer of Wireless Communications
71 Hereford Road, Bayswater, London W2

MARLEY, Bob (1945-1981) Regae Singer
34 Ridgmount Gardens, Camden, London
42 Oakley Street, Chelsea, London

MARSDEN, Gerry (1942-2021) Singer - Gerry and the Pacemakers
8 Menzies Street, Toxteth, Liverpool

MARSDEN, William (1796-1867) Surgeon
(Founder of Royal Marsden Hospital)
65 Lincoln's Inn Fields, London WC2

MARX, Karl (1818-1883)
28 Dean Street, London W1
4 Anderson Street, Chelsea, London
56 Plains of Waterloo, Ramsgate, Kent

MASEFIELD, John (1878-1967) Poet Laureate
The Knapp, The Homend, Ledbury,
30 Maida Avenue, London W2
13 Well Walk, Hampstead, London

MATCHAM, Frank (1854-1920) Theatre architect
10 Haslemere Road, Crouch End, London

MATTHEWS, Stanley (1915-2000) Footballer
Born: 89 Seymour Street, Hanley, Stoke on Trent
The Grange, St Anne's Road, Blackpool

MAUGHAN, William Somerset (1874-1965) Novelist and Playwright
6 Chesterfield Street, London W1

McCARTNEY, Paul (1942-) Musician with "The Beatles"
20 Forthlin Street, Liverpool
57 Wimpole Street, Marylebone, London
7 Cavendish Avenue, St John's Wood, London

McCORMACK, John (1884-1945) Tenor
24 Ferncroft Avenue, Hampstead, London

McDONALD, Ramsey (1836-1937) Prime Minister
9 Howitt Road, Belsize Park, London

McGILL, Donald (1875-1962) Postcard Cartoonist
5 Bennett Park, Blackheath, London SE3

MELBA, Nellie (1861-1931) Operatic Soprano
Coombe House, Devey Close, Kingston upon Thames, London

MELVILLE, Herman (1819-1891) Author, Moby Dick
25 Craven Street, London

MENDELSSOHN, Felix (1809-1847) Classical Composer
4 Hobart Place, Belgravia, London

MERCURY, Freddie (1946-1991) Singer with " Queen"
22 Gladstone Avenue, Feltham, London
12 Stafford Terrace, Kensington, London
1 Logan Place, Kensington, London

MICHAEL, George (1963-2016) Singer
73 Church Lane, East Finchley, London
5 The Grove, Highgate, London
Mill Cottage, Lock Approach, Goring on Thames

MILLAIS, John Everett (1829-1896) Painter
7 Gower Street, Bloomsbury, London WC1E 6HA
83 Gower Street, Bloomsbury, London
2 Palace Gate, Kensington, London

MILLER, Max 1895-1963) Comedian
25 Burlington Street, Brighton
Ashcroft, Kingston Lane, Shoreham-by- Sea, West Sussex
160 Marine Parade, Brighton

MILLIGAN, Spike (1918-2002) Comedy Actor/ Writer
127 Holden Road, Finchley, London
Flat 4, Highview, 77 Highgate Road, Highgate, London
9 Orme Court, London

MILNE, A.A. (1882-1956) Author
13 Mallord Street, London SW3
Cotchford Farm, Hartfield, East Sussex

MONRO, Matt (1930-1985) Singer
1 Dallas Road, Ealing, London

MITFORD, Nancy (1904-1973) Writer
10 Curzon Street, Mayfair, London

MONTGOMERY, Field Marshall (1887-1976)
Oval House, 52-54 Kennington Oval, London SE11 (born here)

MONKHOUSE, Bob (1928-2003) Comedian/ presenter
52 Upper Montague Street, Maryleborne, London W1H 1SJ
Claridges, Eggington, near Leighton Buzzard

MOORE, Bobby (1941-1993) Footballer
43 Waverley Gardens, Barking, London

MOORE, Henry (1898-1986) Sculptor
11a Parkhill Road, Hampstead, London

MORECAMBE, Eric (1926-1984) Comedian "Morecambe and Wise"
85 Torrington Park, London
48 Buxton Street, Morecambe

MORRIS, William (1834-1896) Textile Designer, Artist
Kelmscote Manor, Kelmscote, Oxfordshire
Elm House, 341/343 Forest Road, Walthamstow, London
Red House, Red House Lane, Bexleyheath, London
26 Upper Mall, Hammersmith, London
17 Red Square, Holborn, London

MORRISON, Herbert (1888-1965) Cabinet Minister
55 Archery Road, Eltham, London SE9

MORSE, Samuel (1791-1872) Inventor of Morse Code
141 Cleveland Street, Fitzrovia, London W1

MOUNTBATTEN, Earl of Burma (1900-1979) Last Viceroy of India
2 Wilton Crescent, London SW1

MOZART, Wolfgang Amadeus (1756-1791) Classical Composer
180 Ebury Street, Victoria, London SW1
20 Frith Street, Soho. London

NASH, John (1752-1835) Architect
66 Great Russell Street, Bloomsbury, London

NEHRU, Jawaharlal (1889-1964) First Prime Minister of India
60 Elgin Crescent, Notting Hill, London W11

NELSON, Horatio (1758-1805) British Naval Commander
103 New Bond Street, London W1
147 New Bond Street, Mayfair, London
20 Arlington Street, Mayfair, London

NEWTON, Isaac (1642-1727) Natural Philosopher
87 Jermyn Street, London SW1 (Premises re-built)
Bullingham Mansions, Kensington Church Street, London

NEWTON, Robert (1905-1956) Actor
17 Victoria Street, Shaftsbury, Dorset
The Old Cottage, Whitwell, Hertfordshire

NIGHTINGALE, Florence (1820-1910)
10 South Street, London W1 (Premises re-built)
90 Harley Street, Marylebone, London

NOVELLO, Ivor (1893-1951) Composer
11 Aldwych, London WC2
55 New Bond Street, Mayfair, London

NUREYEV, Rudolf (1938-1993) Ballet Dancer
The Old Farm, 6 Fife Road, East Sheen, London
27 Victoria Road, Kensington, London
Dakota Building, West 72nd Street, New York

ORTON, Joe (1933-1967) Playwright
25 Noel Road, Islington, London
31 Gower Street, Bloomsbury, London
161 West End Lane, West Hampstead, London

ORWELL, George (1903-1950) Novelist
Barnhill Isle, Jura, Argyllshire. 22 Portobello Road, Notting Hill, London
3 Warwick Mansions, 37 Pond Street, Hampstead, London
50 Lawford Road, Kentish Town, London
Kit's Lane, Wallington, Hertfordshire

OSBORNE, John (1929-1994) Playwright
53 Caithness Road, Hammersmith, London

PAGE, Jimmy (1944-) Band Member with "Led Zepplin"
29 Melbury Road, Kensington, London
Boleskine House, Foyers, Loch Ness
Plumpton Place, Lewes, Sussex

PALMERSTON, Henry John Temple (1784-1865) British Prime Minister
Born 20 Queen Anne's Gate, London SW1
4 Carlton Gardens, London SW1
94 Piccadilly, London

PANKHURST, Emmeline (1858-1928) Campaigner for Women's Rights
50 Clarendon Road, Holland Park, London

PANKHURST, Sylvia (1882-1960) Campaigner for Women's Rights
120 Cheyne Walk, Chelsea, London SW10

PARRY, Charles Hubert Hastings (1848-1918) Classical Composer
17 Kensington Square, Kensington, London W8

PAXTON, Joseph (1803-1865) Gardener and Engineer
Chatsworth Estate, Derbyshire

PEEL, Robert (1788-1850) Founder of the Metropolitan Police
16 Upper Grosvenor Street, London W1
7 Eastern Terrace, Brighton, Sussex

PELHAM, Henry (1694-1754) Prime Minister
Wimborne House, 22 Arlington Street, London

PEPYS, Samuel (1633-1703) Diarist
12 Buckingham Street, London WC2

PERCEVAL, Spencer (1762-1812) Prime Minister
59-60 Lincoln's Inn Fields, Holborn, London

PERRY, Fred 91909-1995) Tennis player
223 Pitshanger Lane, Ealing

PEVSNER, Nikolaus (1902-1983) Architectural Historian
2 Wildwood Terrace, Hampstead, London

PISSARRO, Camille (1830-1903) Painter
10 Kew Green/ Gloucester Place, Kew, London

PISSARRO, Lucien (1863-1944) Painter
27 Stamford Brook Road, Chiswick, London W6

PITT, William (the younger) (1759-1806) British Prime Minister
120 Baker Street, London W1

POPE, Alexander (1688-1744) Poet
Mawson Arms PH, 110 Chiswick Lane South, Chiswick, London W4

PRIESTLEY, J.B. (1894-1984) Novelist, Playwright
3 The Grove, Highgate, London N6
Brook Hill House, Newport, Isle of Wight

RAMBERT, Marie (1888-1982) Founder of Ballet Rambert
19 Campden Hill Gardens, Holland Park, London W8

RANK, Joseph Arthur (1888-1972) Film Producer
38 South Street, Mayfair, London

RATTIGAN, Terence (1911-1977) Playwright
100 Cornwall Gardens, Kensington, London

RAVILIOUS, Eric (1903-1942) Artist
48 Upper Mall, Hammesmith, London

REITH, (Lord) John Charles (1889-1971) first Director-General BBC
6 Barton Street, London SW1

RELPH, Harry (1867-1928) Music Hall Comedian ("Little Tich")
93 Shirehall Park, Hendon, London NW4

REYNOLDS, Bruce (1931-2013) Train robber
24 Florian Road, Putney, London SW15
38 Buckmaster road, Battersea, London

REYNOLDS, Joshua (1723-1792) Painter
Fanum House (site of 47) Leicester Square, London WC2
(Premises re-built)

RICHARDS, Gordon (1904-1986) Jockey and Trainer
Duff House, Kintbury, Berkshire

RICHARDS, Keith (1943-) Musician "Rolling Stones"
3 Cheyne Walk, Chelsea, London
Redlands, West Wittering, West Sussex

RICHARDSON, Ralph (1902-1983) Actor
Bedegar's Lea, Kenwood Close, Hampstead, London

ROBESON, Paul (1898-1976) Singer
The Chestnuts, 1 Branch Hill, Camden, London NW3

ROLLS, Charles (1877-1910) Pioneer of Motoring
14-15 Conduit Street, Mayfair, London

ROSSETTI, Dante Gabriel (1828-1882) Poet and Artist
Born 110 Hallam Street, London W1 (Premises re-built)
Lived 16 Cheyne Walk, London SW3
46 Cleveland Street, Fitzrovia, London
17 Red Lion Square, Holborn, London

RUSKIN, John (1819-1900)
26 Herne Hill, London SE24 (Premises re-built)
Brantwood, Coniston, Cumbria

RUTHERFORD, Margaret (1892-1972) Actress
4 Berkeley Place, Wimbledon, London SW19

RUSSELL, Bertrand (1872-1970) Philosopher
34 Russell Chambers, Bury Place, London WC1

SALISBURY, Robert Gascoyne Cecil (1830-1903)
British Prime Minister
21 Fitzroy Square, London W1

SARGENT, Malcolm (1895-1967) Classical Conductor
Flat 9, Albert Hall Mansions, Kensington Gore, London SW7

SAYERS, Dorothy (1893-1957) Author
24 Great James Street, Holborn, London

SCARFE, Gerald (1936-) Cartoonist
10 Cheyne Walk, Chelsea, London SW3 5QZ

SCOTT, George Gilbert (1811-1878) Architect
Admiral's House, Admiral's Walk, Hampstead, London NW3

SCOTT, Robert Falcon (1868-1912) Antarctic Explorer
56 Oakley Street, Chelsea, London SW3
174 Buckingham Palace Road, Victoria, London

SCOTT, Walter (1771-1832) Author
Abbotsford House, Melrose, Scotland
76 Jermyn Street, Mayfair, London

SEACOLE, Mary (1805-1881) Nurse Crimean War
14 Soho Square, London W1

SELLARS, Peter (1925-1980) Comedy Actor
10 Muswell Hill Road, Muswell Hill, London

SHACKLETON, Ernest Henry (1874-1922) Antarctic Explorer
12 Westwood Hill, London SE26
14 Milnthorpe Road, Eastbourne, Sussex

SHAW, George Bernard (1856-1950) Author
29 Fitzroy Square, London W1
4 Whitehall Court, Westminster, London

SHELTON, Anne (1923-1994) Singer
142 Court Lane, Dulwich, London

SHELLEY, Mary (1797-1851) Novelist
87 Marchmont Street, Bloomsbury, London
24 Chester Square, Belgravia, London

SHERATON, Thomas (1751-1806) Furniture Designer
163 Wardour Street, London W1

SIBELIUS, Jean (1865-1957) Classical Composer
15 Gloucester Walk, Kensington, London W8

SICKERT, Walter (1860-1942) Painter
6 Mornington Crescent, London NW1

SIM, Alastair (1900-1976) Actor
8 Frognal Gardens, Hampstead, London

SITWELL, Edith (1887-1964) Poet
Greenhill, Hampstead High Street, London NW3
20 Keats Grove, Hampstead, London

SLOANE, Hans (1660-1753) Physician and Benefactor of British Museum
4 Bloomsbury Place, London WC1

SMITH, W.H. (1825-1891) Bookseller and Statesman
12 Hyde Park Street, London W2

SOANE, John (1753-1857) Architect
13 Lincoln's Inn Fields, London

SOPWITH, Thomas (1888-1989) Aviator and Aircraft Manufacturer
46 Green Street, Mayfair, London W1

SPENCE, Basil (1907-1976) Architect
1 Canonbury Place, Islington, London

SPRINGFIELD, Dusty (1939-1999) Singer
38 Aubrey Walk, Kensington, London
Little Hill, Henley-on Thames, Berkshire

THE HERITAGE FOUNDATION
DUSTY
SPRINGFIELD
O.B.E.
1939-1999
Singer
Lived here
1968-1972

STARR, Ringo (1940-) Drummer "The Beatles"
10 Admiral Grove, Dingle, Liverpool
9 Madryn Street, Dingle, Liverpool
Round Hill, Compton Avenue, Highgate, London
Sunny Heights, St George's Hill, Weybridge, Surrey
Tittenhurst Park, Sunninghill, Ascot, Berkshire

STEELE, Tommy (1936-) Singer, Entertainer
Nickleby House, Dockhead, Bermondsey

STEPHENSON, George (1781-1848) Civil & Mechanical Engineer
Tapton House, Tapton, Chesterfield

STEPHENSON, Robert (1803-1859) Engineer
35 Gloucester Square, London W2

STEVENSON, Robert Louis (1850-1894) Novelist
7 Mount Vernon, Hampstead, London

STEWART, Rod (1945-) Pop singer
507 Archway Road, Highgate, London

STOKER, Bram (1847-1912) Author of "Dracula"
18 St Leonard's Terrace, London SW3

STOPES, Marie (1880-1958) Promoter of birth control
28 Cintra Park, Crystal Palace, London

STRINGFELLOW. Peter (1940-2018) Entertainment entrepreneur
Andover Street, Pitsmoor, Sheffield
Marshall Street, Pitsmoor, Sheffield

SUCHET, John (1944-) Broadcaster
Chiltern Court, Baker Street, London

SWANN, Donald (1923-1994) Performer of comic songs
1 Scarsdale Villas, Kensington, London

SYKES, Eric (1923-2012) Comedian
36 Leslie Street, Oldham, Manchester
9 Orme Court, Bayswater

TATE, Henry (1819-1899) Sugar Magnate
42 Hamilton Square, Birkenhead, Wirral

TAUBER, Richard (1891-1948) Singer
297 Park West, Edgware Road, London

TENNYSON, Alfred (1809-1892) Poet
9 Upper Belgrave Street, London SW1

TERRY, Ellen (1847-1928) Actress
22 Barkston Gardens, Earls Court, London SW5

THACKERAY, William Makepeace (1811-1863) Novelist
2 Palace Green, Kensington, London W8
36 Onslow Square, Kensington, London
16 Young Street, Kensington, London

THATCHER, Margaret (1925-2013) Politician
93 Eaton Square, Belgravia, London
73 Chester Square, Belgravia, London
19 Flood Street, Chelsea, London

THOMAS, Dylan (1914-1953) Poet
54 Delancey Street, Camden Town, London

THOMAS, Terry (1911-1990) Comic Actor
11 Queens Gate Mews, Kensington, London

THOMSON, William (1824-1907) (Lord Kelvin) Physicist
15 Eaton Place, Belgravia, London

THORNDIKE, Sybil (1882-1976) Actress
6 Carlyle Square, Chelsea, London

TOLKEIN, J.R.R (1892-1973) Author
20 Northmore Road, Oxford

TRAVERS, Pamela Lyndon (1899-1996) Author "Mary Poppins"
50 Smith Street, Chelsea, London

TRINDER, Tommy (1909-1989) Comedian
Born: 54 Wellfield Road, Streatham, London

TROLLOPE, Anthony (1815-1882) Novelist
39 Montagu Square, London W1

TURNER, J.M.W. (1775-1851) Painter
21 Maiden Lane, Covent Garden, London
40 Sandycombe Road, Twickenham, London
119 Cheyne Walk, Chelsea, London

TUSSAUD, Marie (1761-1850) Artist in Wax
24 Wellington Road, St John's Wood, London NW8

TURING, Alan (1912-1954) Mathematician, Cryptographer
Copper Folly, Ashtree Close, Prestbury, Macclesfield
2 Warrington Crescent, Maida Vale, London

TWAIN, Mark (Samuel Langhorne Clemens) (1835-1910) Writer
23 Tedworth Square, London SW3

TWIGGY (Leslie Hornby) (1949-) Model
23 St Raphael's Way Neasden, London

VAN GOGH, Vincent (1853-1890) Painter
87 Hackford Road, London SW9

VAUGHAN WILLIAMS, Ralph (1872-1958)
10 Hanover Terrace, Regent's Park, London NW1
13 Cheyne Walk, Chelsea, London

VICKERS, Edward (1804-1897) Steel Industrialist
Tapton Hall, Shore Lane, Sheffield

WALL, Max (1908-1990) Comedian
Born: Glenshaw Mansions, Mowll Street, Kennington, London

WALLACE, Barnes (1887-1979) Designer of Aeroplanes and "Bouncing Bomb"
241 New Cross Road, London SE14

WALLACE, Edgar (1875-1932) Writer
6 Tressillian Crescent, London SE4

WALPOLE, Robert (1676-1745) British Prime Minister
5 Arlington Street, London SW1

WALTON, William (1902-1983) Composer
Lowndes Cottage, 8 Lowndes Place, Belgravia, London

WARD, Stephen Thomas (1912-1963) Osteopath
17 Wimpole Mews, Marylebone, London

WATERHOUSE, Alfred (1830-1905) Architect
61 New Cavendish Street, Marylebone, London

WATERHOUSE, John William (1849-1917) Artist
10 Hall Road, St John's Wood, London NW8

WATTS, Charlie (1941 - 2021) Drummer, Rolling Stones
Ivor Court, Gloucester Place, London

WAUGH, Evelyn (1903-1966) Writer
145 North End Road, Golder's Green, London NW11

WELLCOME, Henry (1853-1936) Founder of Wellcome Trust
6 Gloucester Gate, Regents Park, London

WELLESLEY, Arthur (1769-1852) 1st Duke of Wellington
Apsley House, Hyde Park, London

WELLS, H.G. (1866-1946) Writer
13 Hanover Terrace, London NW1
17 Church Row, Hampstead, London

WESLEY, John (1703-1791)
The Old Rectory, Epworth, Lincolnshire
47 City Road, Islington, London

WHEELER, Mortimer (1890-1976) Archaeologist
27 Whitcomb Street, London

WHISTLER, James Abbot McNeill (1834-1903) Painter
96 Cheyne Walk, London SW10

WILBERFORCE, William (1759-1833) Campaigner against Slavery
Site of Broomwood House (now demolished)
111 Broomwood Road, London
44 Cadogan Place, London SW1

WILDE, Oscar O'Flahertie Wills (1854-1900) Dramatist
34 Tite Street, Chelsea, London SW3

WILLIAMS, Kenneth (1926-1988) Comedy Actor ("Carry On" films)
Born: 11 Bingfield Street, Islington, London
57 Marchmont Street, Bloomsbury, London
8 Marlborough House, Osnaburgh Street, London (now demolished)
Farley Court, Allsop Place, London

WILLIAMS, Ralph Vaughan (1872-1958) Classical Composer
10 Hanover Terrace, Regents Park London

WILSON, Harold (1916-1995) Prime Minister
Fitzwilliam House, Flat 4, Little Green, Richmond, London

WISDOM, Norman (1915-2010) Comedy Actor
91 Fernhead Road, London W9

WISE, Ernie (1925-1999) Comedian
6 Atlanta Street, Leeds LS13
Dorney Reach, Maidenhead, Berkshire

WODEHOUSE, P.G. (1881-1975) Writer
17 Dunraven Street, London W1

WOOD, Henry (1869-1944) Musician
4 Elsworthy Road, NW3

WOOD, Ronnie (1947-) Guitarist "Rolling Stones"
Holmwood House, Richmond Park, London

WOOLF, Virginia (1882-1941) Writer
22 Hyde Park Gate, London
46 Gordon Square, Bloomsbury, London
29 Fitzroy Square, London W1

WORTH. Harry (1917- 1989) Comedian
47 Fitzwilliam Street, Hoyland Common, Barnsley

WREN, Christopher (1632-1723) Architect
The Old Court House, Hampton Court Green, East Molesey,
Richmond upon Thames
49 Bankside, Southwark, London

WYMAN, Bill (1936-) Musician "Rolling Stones"
36 Blenheim Road, Putney, London

WYNDHAM, Charles (1837-1919) Actor, Manager
20 York Terrace East, Regent's Park, London

ZOFFANY, Johann (1733-1810) Artist
65 Strand on the Green, Chiswick, London

ZOLA, Emile (1840-1902) French Novelist
Queen's Hotel, 122 Church Road, Upper Norwood, London SE19

PREVIOUS HOMES OF FAMOUS PEOPLE (USA)

ANDREWS, Julie (1935 -) Singer, Actress
27944 Pacific Coast Highway, Malibu

ASTAIRE, Fred (1899-1987) Dancer
806 Rodeo Drive, Beverley Hills, L.A
1155 Ysidro Drive, Beverley Hills, L.A

BACALL, Lauren (1924-2014) Actress
2707 Benedict Canyon Drive, Beverley Hills, L.A
75 Bank Street, New York
Dakota Building, West 72nd Street, New York

BALL, Lucille (1911-1989) Comedy Actress
1000 N. Roxbury Drive, Beverley Hills, L.A

BECKHAM, David (1975-) Footballer
1015 N, Roxbury Drive, Beverley Hills, L.A

BENNY, Jack (1894-1974) Comedian
1002 N. Roxbury Drive, Beverley Hills, L.A
1016 Benedict Canyon Drive, Beverley Hills, L.A

BERGMAN, Ingrid (1915-1982) Actress
1220 Benedict Canyon Drive, Beverley Hills, L.A
150 Central Park South, N.Y

BERLIN, Irving (1888-1989) Composer
17 Beekman Place, N.Y

BERNSTEIN, Leonard (1918-1990) Composer
Dakota Building, West 72nd Street, New York

BOGART, Humphrey (1899-1957) Actor
2707 Benedict Canyon Drive, Beverley Hills, L.A
434 E 52nd Street , N.Y

BONO, Sonny (1935-1998) Singer, Politician
1014 N. Roxbury Drive, Beverley Hills, L.A

BRANDO, Marlon (1924-2004) Actor
131 S. Bedford Drive, Beverley Hills, L.A

CANTOR, Eddie (1892-1964) Entertainer
1012 N. Roxbury Drive, Beverley Hills, L.A

CARLISLE, Belinda (1958-) Singer
1843 Benedict Canyon Drive, Beverley Hills, L.A

CHER, (1946-) Singer
2727 Benedict Canyon Drive, Beverley Hills, L.A

COCKER, Joe (1944-2014) Singer
Mad Dog Ranch, Crawford, Colorado

COLLINS, Phil (1951 -) Singer
9401 Sunset Blvd, Beverley Hills, L.A

COOPER, Gary (1901-1961) Actor
728 Rodeo Drive, Beverley Hills, L.A

CRAWFORD, Joan (1904-1977) Actress
36 Sutton Place South, N.Y

DIETRICH, Marlene (1901-1992) Actress
913 Bedford Drive, Beverley Hills, L.A

DISNEY, Walt (1901-1966) Animator, Entrepreneur
355 Carolwood Drive, Beverley Hills, L.A

DYLAN, Bob (1941 -) Singer, Songwriter
29400 Bluewater Road, Malibu

FALK Peter (1927-2011) Actor
1004 N. Roxbury Drive, Beverley Hills, L.A

FAYE, Alice (1915-1998) Actress
1110 Benedict Canyon Drive, Beverley Hills, L.A

FISHER, Carrie (1956-2016) Actress
1700 Coldwater Canyon, Beverley Hills, L.A

FLEETWOOD, Mick (1947-) Singer, Musician
11435 Bellagio Road, Bel Air, L.A

FORD, Harrison (1942-) Actor
1420 Braeridge Drive, Beverley Hills. L.A
101 Central Park West, N.Y

GABOR, Zsa Zsa (1917-2016) Actress, Socialite
938 Bel Air Road, Beverley Hills, L.A

GARBO, Greta (1905-1990) Actress
904 Bedford Drive, Beverley Hills, L.A

GARDNER, Ava (1922-1990) Actress
904 Bedford Drive, Beverley Hills, L.A

GARFUNKEL, Art (1941-) Singer
120 E 87st Street, N.Y

GARLAND, Judy (1922-1969)
Dakota Building, West 72nd Street, New York

GERE, Richard (1949-) Actor
10790 Bellagio Road, Bel Air, L.A

GERSHWIN (1898-1937) Composer
1019 N. Roxbury Drive, Beverley Hills, L.A

GERSHWIN, Ira (1896-1983) Lyricist
1021 N. Roxbury Drive, Beverley Hills, L.A

GRABLE, Betty (1916-1973) Actress
1015 N. Roxbury Drive, Beverley Hills, L.A

GRANGER, Stewart (1913-1993) Actor
800 Bel Air Road, Beverley Hills, L.A

GRANT, Cary (1904-1986) Actor
10615 Bellagio Road, Bel Air, L.A
2850 Benedict Canyon Drive, Beverley Hills, L.A

HARDY, Oliver (1892-1957) Comedy Actor
621 Alta Drive, Beverley Hills, L.A

HARRISON, Rex (1908-1990) Actor
904 Bedford Drive, Beverley Hills, L.A

HAWN, Goldie (1945-) Actress
301 W 57th Street, N.Y

HOFFMAN, Dustin (1937-) Actor
145 Central Park West, N.Y

HUGHES, Howard (1905-1976) Business Magnate
10590 Bellagio Road, Bel Air, L.A

KEATON, Diane (1946-) Actress
1015 N. Roxbury Drive, Beverley Hills, L.A

KELLY, Gene (1912-1996) Entertainer
904 Bedford Drive, Beverley Hills, L.A
725 Rodeo Drive, Beverley Hills, L.A

KELLY, Grace (1929-1982) Actress
10590 Bellagio Road, Bel Air, L.A

KENNEDY ONASIS, Jacqueline (1929-1994) First Lady
1040 5th Avenue, N.Y

KING, Billie Jean (1943-) Tennis Player
101 W 79th Street, N.Y

KISSINGER, Henry (1923-) Politician
435 E 52nd Street, N.Y

LANZA, Mario (1921-1959) Singer
500 Bel Air Road, Beverley Hills, L.A

LAUREL, Stan (1890-1965) Comedy Actor
718 North Bedford Drive, Beverley Hills, L.A
111 Franklin Street, Santa Monica, L.A
25406 Malibu Road, Malibu, California

LEE, Peggy (1920-2002) Singer
11404 Bellagio Road, Bel Air, L.A

LENNON (1940-1980) Musician "The Beatles"
Dakota Building, West 72nd Street, New York

LIBERACE, (1919-1987) Entertainer
1441 Kaweah Road, Palm Springs

LLOYD, Harold (1893-1971) Comic Actor
1225 Benedict Canyon Drive, Beverley Hills, L.A

LOPEZ, Jennifer (1969-) Singer
1014 N. Roxbury Drive, Beverley Hills, L.A

MADONNA (1958-) Singer
1015 N. Roxbury Drive, Beverley Hills, L.A

MANILOW, Barry (1943-) Singer
5443 Beethoven Street, Culver, L.A
146 Central Park West, N.Y

MARX, Chico (1887-1961) Comedy Actor
932 Bedford Drive, Beverley Hills, L.A

MARX, Groucho (1890-1977) Comedy Actor
179 East 93rd Street, New York
1083 N. Hillcrest Drive, Beverley Hills, L.A

MARX, Harpo (1888-1964) Comedy Actor
179 East 93rd Street, New York

MARX, Zeppo (1901-1979) Comedy Actor
902 Bedford Drive, Beverley Hill,. L.A

McENROE, John, (1959 -) Tennis Player
211 Central Park West, N.Y

MEYER, Louis, B (1884-1957) Film Producer
910 Benedict Canyon Drive, Beverley Hills, L.A

MILLAND, Ray (1907-1986) Actor
618 Alta Drive, Beverley Hills, L.A

MILLAR, Ann (1923-2004) Dancer
618 Alta Drive, Beverley Hills, Los Angeles
910 Benedict Canyon Drive, Beverley Hills, L.A

MONTGOMERY, Elizabeth (1933-1995) Actress
911 North Roxbury Drive, Beverley Hills, L.A

MONROE. Marilyn (1926-1962) Actress
8573 Holloway Drive, West Hollywood
12305 Fifth Helena Drive, Brentwood, L.A

MURPHY, Eddie (1961-) Actor
2727 Benedict Canyon Drive, Beverley Hills, L.A

NEWMAN, Paul (1925-2008) Actor
907 Whittier Drive, Beverley Hills, L.A

NICHOLSON, Jack (1937 -) Actor
12850 Mulholland Drive, Beverley Hills, L.A

NUREYEV, Rudolf (1938-1993) Ballet Dancer
Dakota Building, West 72nd Street, New York

PECK, Gregory (1916-2003) Actor
375 N.Carolwood Drive, L.A

POLANSKI, Roman (1933-) Film Director/ Producer
1200 N. Alta Loma Road, Beverley Hills, L.A

PRESLEY, Elvis (1935-1977) Singer
Graceland Mansion Estates, Memphis, Tennessee
10590 Bellagio Road, Bel Air, L.A

PREVIN, Andre (1929-2019) Musician, Conductor
304 S. Bedford Drive, Beverley Hills, L.A

PRICE, Vincent (1911-1993) Actor
1815 Benedict Canyon Drive, Beverley Hills, L.A

RANIER, Prince (1923-2005) Monaco Monarch
10590 Bellagio Road, Bel Air, L.A

RODDENBERRY, Gene (1921-1991) Television Producer
10615 Bellagio Road, Bel Air, L.A

ROGERS, Ginger (1911-1995) Dancer
906 N. Roxbury Drive, Beverley Hills, L.A
425 E 58th Street, N.Y

ROSS, Diana (1944 -) Singer
701 Maple Drive, Beverley Hills, L.A

SIMMONS, Gene (1949-) Singer
2650 Benedict Canyon Drive, Beverley Hills, L.A

SINATRA, Frank (1915-1998) Singer
Born: 45 Monroe Street, New York
1148 East Alejo Road, Palm Springs
841 Garden Street, Hoboken,
New Jersey
915 Foothill Road, Beverley Hills, L.A

46

SPRINGSTEEN, Bruce (1949-) Singer
1224 Benedict Canyon Drive, L.A

STANWYCK, Barbara (1907-1990) Actress
807 Rodeo Drive, Beverley Hills, L.A

STARR, Ringo (1940-) Musician
904 Bedford Drive, Beverley Hills, L.A

STEWART, Jimmy (1908-1997) Actor
918 N. Roxbury Drive, Beverley Hills, L.A

STREISAND, Barbra (1942-) Singer
904 Bedford Drive, Beverley Hills, L.A
320 Central Park West, N.Y

SULLIVAN, Ed (1901-1974) TV Celebrity
621 Alta Drive, Beverley Hills, L.A

TAYLOR, Elizabeth (1932-2011) Actress
700 Nimes Road, Bel Air, L.A
315 E72nd Street, N.Y

TAYLOR, Robert (1911-1969) Actor
807 Rodeo Drive, Beverley Hills, L.A

TRACY, Spencer (1900-1967) Actor
1023 N. Roxbury Drive, Beverley Hills, L.A

TRUMP, Donald (1946-) President
725 5th Avenue, N.Y

TURNER, Lana (1921-1995) Actress
730 Bedford Drive, Beverley Hills, L.A

VALENTINO, Rudolph (1895-1926) Actor
1436 Bella Drive, Beverley Hills, L.A

VANDERBILT, Gloria (1924-2019) Heiress, Socialite
10 Gracie Square, N.Y

WILSON, Brian (1942-) Singer
10452 Bellagio Road, Bel Air, L.A

GRAVES OF FAMOUS PEOPLE (UK)

Alphabetical Order

Where there is a grave to view it is marked thus :- (G)
Where the deceased has been cremated and there is a
memorial to view it is marked thus :- (M)

ADAM, Robert (1728-1792) Architect (G)
      Westminster Abbey, London

ADAMS, Douglas (1952-2001) Writer, dramatist (G)
      Highgate Cemetery (East), London

ADLER, Larry (1914-2000) Musician – Harmonica (M)
      Golders Green Crematorium, London

AINSWORTH, Alyn (1924-1990) Composer (M)
      East Finchley Cemetery and Crematorium, East Finchley, London

ALBERT, Prince (1819-1861) English Royalty (G)
      Frogmore, Windsor

ALCOCK, John (1892-1919) First non-stop transatlantic flight crossing (G)
      Southern Cemetery, Chorlton-Cum-Hardy, Manchester

ALFRED, The Great (849-899) Anglo Saxon Monarch (M)
      Winchester Cathedral, Winchester

AMIS, Kingsley (1922-1995) Author (G)
      Golders Green Crematorium, London

ANNE I (1665-1714) British Monarch (G)
      Westminster Abbey, London

ANNE of Cleves (1515-1557) British Monarch (G)
      Westminster Abbey, London

ARKWRIGHT, Richard (1732-1792) Inventor/ Industrialist (G)
      St Mary Churchyard, Cromford, Derbyshire

ASHCROFT, Peggy (1907-1991) Actress (M)
      Westminster Abbey, London

ASHMOLE, Elias (1617-1692) Scientist (G)
St Mary Churchyard, Lambeth, London

ASHTON, Frederick (1904-1988) Ballet Choreographer (G)
St Mary the Virgin Churchyard, Yaxley, Suffolk

ASKEY, Arthur (1900-1982) Comedian (G)
Putney Vale Cemetery and Crematorium London

ATTLEE, Clement (1883-1967) British Prime Minister (G)
Westminster Abbey, London

AUSTEN, Jane (1775-1817) Novelist (G)
Winchester Cathedral, Winchester

BABBAGE, Charles (1791-1871) Scientist/ Mathematician (G)
Kensal Green Cemetery London

BACH, Johann Christian (1735-1782) Classical Composer (M)
St Pancras Old Churchyard, London

BACON, Francis (1561-1626) Philosopher (G)
St Michael's Churchyard, St Albans

BAIRD, John Logie (1888-1946) Engineer and Inventor
Helensburgh Cemetery, Helensburgh, Argyll and Bute, Scotland

BAKER, Hylda (1904-1986) Entertainer (M)
Twickenham Cemetery, Whitton, London

BALDWIN, Stanley (1867-1947) Politician (G)
Golders Green Crematorium (ashes taken to Worcester Cathedral)

BARBIROLLI, John (1899-1970) Orchestral Conductor (G)
St Mary's R.C.Cemetery, Kensal Green, London

BARKER, Ronnie (1929-2005) Actor/ Comedian {M}
Banbury Crematorium, Banbury

BASSETT, George (1818-1886) Founder of Liquorice Allsorts (G)
General Cemetery Road, Sheffield

BATES, Alan (1934-2003) Actor (G)
St Mary's Churchyard, Bradbourne, Derbyshire

BAZELGETTE, Joseph William (1819-1891) Victorian Engineer (G)
St Mary's Churchyard, Wimbledon, London

BEATON, Cecil (1904-1980) Photographer (G)
 All Saints Churchyard, Broad Chalke, Wiltshire

BECK, James (1929-1973) Actor (Dads Army) (M)
 Putney Vale Cemetery and Crematorium

BECKET, Thomas (1118-1170) Archbishop of Canterbury (M)
 Canterbury Cathedral, Canterbury

BECKINSALE, Richard (1947-1979) Actor (M)
 Mortlake Crematorium London

BEECHAM, Thomas (1879-1961) Classical Orchestra Conductor (G)
 St Peter's Churchyard, Limpsfield,

BENNETT, William Sterndale (1816-1875) Classical Composer (G)
 Westminster Abbey, London

BENTINCK, William Henry Cavendish (1738-1809) Prime Minister (M)
 East Finchley Cemetery and Crematorium, East Finchley, London

BESSEMER, Henry (1813-1898) Inventor (Steel Industry) (G)
 West Norwood Cemetery and Crematorium, London

BETJEMAN, John (1906-1984) Poet (G)
 St Enodoc Churchyard, Trebetherick, Cornwall

BEVIN, Ernest (1881-1951) Politician (M)
 Westminster Abbey, London

BICKERSTAFFE, John (1848-1930) Chairman of Blackpool Tower (G)
 Layton Cemetery, Blackpool

BILK, Acker (1929-2014) Musician (G)
 All Saints Churchyard, Publow, Somerset

BLACK, Cilla (1943-2015) Singer (G)
 Allerton Cemetery, Allerton, Liverpool

BLAKE, William (1757-1827) Poet/Artist (G)
 Bunhill Fields, City Road, London

BLISS, Arthur (1891-1975) Composer (G)
 Old Mortlake Cemetery, London

BLONDIN, Charles (1824-1897) Tightrope Walker (G)
 Kensal Green Cemetery London

BOLAN, Marc (1947-1977) Singer (T-Rex) (M)
    Golders Green Crematorium, London

BOLEYN, Anne (1501-1536) Queen Consort, Second wife of Henry VIII (G)
    Church of St Peter-ad Vincula, Tower of London

BONHAM, John (1948-1980) Rock Musician with "Led Zepplin" (G)
    St Michael Churchyard, Rushock, Worcestershire

BOOTH, William (1829-1912) Founder of Salvation Army (G)
    Abney Park Cemetery, Stoke Newington

BOSENQUET, Reginald (1932-1984) Newscaster (G)
    Putney Vale Cemetery and Crematorium, London

BRAMWELL, Wilfred (1912-1985) Actor (Memorial tree)
    Streatham Park Cemetery and Crematorium, Streatham, London

BRESSLAW, Bernard (1934-1993) Actor (Carry-On films) (M)
    Golders Green Crematorium London

BRITTEN, Benjamin (1913-1976) Classical Composer (G)
    St Peter and St Paul Churchyard, Aldeburgh, Suffolk

BRONOWSKI, Jacob (1908-1974) Scientist and broadcaster (G)
    Highgate Cemetery (West), London

BRONTE, Anne (1820-1849) Author (G)
    St Mary Churchyard, Scarborough, Yorkshire

BRONTE, Charlotte (1816-1855) Novelist (G)
    St Michael and All Angels Churchyard, Haworth, Yorkshire

BROWN, Janet (1923-2011) Actress (G)
    Danehill Cemetery, Danehill, Wealden, East Sussex

BROWN, John (1816-1896) Steel Industrialist (G)
    All Saints Churchyard, Ecclesall, Sheffield

BROWN, Lancelot "Capability" (1716-1783) Landscape Designer (G)
    St Peter and St Paul Churchyard, Fenstanton, Cambridgeshire

BROWNING, Robert (1812-1889) Poet (G)
    Westminster Abbey, London

BRUNEL, Isambard Kingdom (1806-1859) Civil Engineer (G)
    Kensal Green Cemetery London

BUNYAN, John (1628-1688) Writer (G)
Bunhill Fields, City Road, London

BUSBY, Matt (1909-1994) British Football Manager (G)
Southern Cemetery, Chorlton Cum Hardy, Manchester

BUTLIN, Billy (1899-1980) Holiday Camp Entrepreneur (G)
St John's Church, St John, Jersey

BUTTERWORTH, Peter (1919-1979) Actor (Carry-On series) (G)
Danehill Cemetery, Danehill, Wealden, East Sussex

BYRON, Lord George Gordon (1788-1824) Poet (G)
St Mary Magdalene Church, Hucknall, Nottinghamshire

CADBURY, John (1801-1899) Chocolate Manufacturer
(Founder of Cadbury's) (G) Witton Cemetery, Birmingham

CADBURY, George (1839-1922) Chocolate Maker
Friends Meeting House Burial Ground, Bourneville, Staffordshire

CAMPBELL, Donald (1921-1967) Sportsman (G)
Coniston Graveyard, Coniston, Lake District

CAPSTICK, Tony (1944-2003) Actor, Comedian (M)
Rotherham Crematorium, Rotherham

CAIROLI, Charlie (1910-1980) Clown and Musician (rose bed)
Carleton Crematorium Blackpool

CALLAGHAN, James (1912-2005) Prime Minister (M)
Ashes scattered at base of Peter Pan statue,
Great Ormond Street Hospital

CANUTE, KING (995-1035) English Monarch (G)
Winchester Cathedral, Winchester

CARSON, Violet (1898-1983) Actress (Coronation Street) (M)
Carleton Crematorium Blackpool

CARTER, Henry Vandyke (1831-1897) Surgeon, Anatomical Artist (G)
Dean Road Cemetery, Scarborough

CARTER, Howard (1874-1939) Scientist/ Archaeologist (G)
Putney Vale Cemetery and Crematorium

CHAMBERLAIN, Neville (1869-1940) Politician (M)
Golders Green Crematorium, London

Alan Bates

Donald Campbell

Henry Boot

Samuel Cunard

CHAMPION, Harry (1865-1942) Music Hall singer (G)
East Finchley Cemetery, East Finchley, London

CHANTREY, Francis (1782-1841) Sculptor (G)
Norton Churchyard, Sheffield

CHARLES I, (1600-1649) English Monarch (G)
St George's Chapel, Windsor, London

CHARLES II, English Monarch (1630-1685) (G)
Westminster Abbey, London

CHAUCER, Geoffrey (1342-1400) Author (G)
Westminster Abbey, London

CHEVALIER, Albert (1861-1923) Music Hall Singer/Comedian (G)
Abney Park Cemetery, Stoke Newington

CHRISTIE, Agatha (1890-1976) Author (G)
St Mary's Churchyard, Cholsey, Oxfordshire

CHURCHILL, Winston (1874-1965) British Prime Minister (G)
St Martin Churchyard, Bladon, Oxfordshire

CLARK, Jim (1936-1968) Racing driver (G)
Chirnside Parish Church cemetery, Chirnside, Scotland

CLARK, Ossie (1942-1996) Fashion Designer (G)
Kensal Green Cemetery London

CLITHEROE, Jimmy (1921-1973) Comedian (M)
Carleton Crematorium Blackpool

COATES, Eric (1886-1957) Composer (M)
Golders Green Crematorium, London

COBORN, Charles (1852-1945) Music Hall Singer (G)
Brompton Cemetery, London

COGAN, Alma (1932-1966) Singer (G)
Bushey Jewish Cemetery London

CONNOLLY, Brian (1945-1997) Singer {The Sweet} {M}
Breakspear Crematorium, Ruislip, London

CONSTABLE, John (1776-1837) Artist (G)
St John at Hampstead, London

CORBETT, Harry H. (1925-1982) Actor (G)
        St Michael the Archangel Churchyard, Penhurst, East Sussex

CRADDOCK, Fannie (1909-1994) TV Cook/ Celebrity (M)
        Eastbourne Crematorium, Eastbourne

CRUFT, Charles (1852-1938) Founder of dog show (G)
        Highgate Cemetery (West), London

CUNARD, Samuel (1787-1865) Founder of Cunard Line (G)
        Brompton Cemetery, London

11th DUKE of DEVONSHIRE {Andrew Robert Buxton Cavendish}
(1920-2004) (G) St Peter Churchyard, Edensor, Chatsworth, Derbyshire

DAHL, Roald (1916-1990) Novelist (G) St Peter and St Paul Churchyard,
        Great Missenden, Buckinghamshire

DANDO, Jill (1961-1999) Journalist and T.V.Presenter (G)
        Ebdon Road Cemetery and Crematorium, Weston-super-Mare,
        Somerset

DARWIN, Charles (1809-1882) Scientist, Naturalist (G)
        Westminster Abbey, London

DAWSON, Les (1931-1993) Comedian (M)
        Lytham Park Cemetery and Crematorium, Blackpool

DAY, Robin (1923-2000) Broadcaster (M)
        Church of Candida and Holy Cross, Whitchurch Canonicorum,
        Dorset

DEKKER, Desmond (1942-2006) Reggae Musician (G)
        Streatham Park Cemetery/ Crematorium

DEFOE, Daniel (1661-1731) Author (G)
        Bunhill Fields, City Road, London

DELIUS, Frederick (1862-1934) Classical Composer (G)
        St Peter's Churchyard, Limpsfield,

DIANA, Princess of Wales (1961-1997) (G)
        Althorpe House Estate, Northamptonshire

DIBNAH, Fred (1938-2004) Steeplejack, TV personality (G)
        Tonge Cemetery, Bolton

DICKENS, Charles (1812-1870) Author (G)
        Westminster Abbey, London

DIMBLEBY, Richard (1913-1965) TV Presenter (M)
Westminster Abbey

DODD, Ken (1927-2018) Comedian (G)
Allerton Cemetery, Liverpool

DORS, Diana (1931-1984) Actress and Entertainer (G)
Sunningdale Catholic Cemetery

DOYLE, Arthur Conan (1859-1930) Author (G)
All Saints Churchyard, Minstead, Hampshire

DUKE, Ronnie (- 1981) Entertainer (with Ricki Lee) (G)
All Saints Church, Cawthorne, Barnsley

DU PRE, Jacqueline (1945-1987) Cellist (G)
Golders Green Jewish Cemetery, London

EDWARD III (1312-1377) English Monarch (G)
Westminster Abbey, London

EDWARD VII (1841-1910) British Monarch (G)
St George's Chapel, Windsor, London

EDWARD VIII (1894-1972) British Monarch (G)
Frogmore, Windsor

EINSTEIN, Albert (1879-1955) Scientist
Ashes scattered in grounds Institute of Advanced Study
Princeton, New Jersey

ELGAR, Edward (1857-1934) Classical Composer   (G)
St Wulstan's Church, Little Malvern

ELIOT, George (Mary Anne Evans) (1819-1880) Writer (G)
Highgate Cemetery (East), London

ELIOT, T.S.(1888-1965) Poet (G)
Golders Green Crematorium, London

ELIZABETH I (1533-1603) English Monarch (G)
Westminster Abbey, London

ELEN, Gus (1863-1940) Music Hall Singer/ Comedian (G)
Streatham Park Cemetery, London

ELIZABETH, Windsor (1900-2002) Mother to Elizabeth II (G)
St George's Chapel, Windsor

ELLINGTON, Ray (1916-1985) Jazz Musician (M)
Golders Green Crematorium, London

EMERY, Dick (1917-1983) Comedian
Mortlake Crematorium, London

EPSTEIN, Brian (1934-1967) The Beatles Manager (G)
Long Lane Jewish Cemetery, Aintree, Liverpool

EPSTEIN, Jacob (1880-1959) Sculptor (G)
Putney Vale Cemetery and Crematorium, London

EVANS, Norman (1901-1962) Comedian (G)
Carleton Cemetery, Blackpool

FARADAY, Michael (1791-1867) Chemist and Physicist (G)
Highgate Cemetery (West), London

FERRIER, Kathleen (1912-1953) Opera Singer (M)
Golders Green Crematorium, London

FIRTH, Mark (1819-1880) Steel Industrialist (G)
General Cemetery, Sheffield

FISHER, Geoffrey (1887-1972) Archbishop (M)
St Andrew Churchyard, Trent, West Dorset

FLANAGAN, Bud (1896-1968) Entertainer (M)
Golders Green Crematorium, London

FLEMING, Alexander (1881-1955) Scientist (M)
St Pauls Cathedral, London

FLEMING, Ian (1908-1964) Author (G)
St James's Churchyard, Sevenhampton, Gloucestershire

FOOT, Michael (1913-2010) Politician (M)
Golders Green Crematorium, London

FOOT, Paul (1937-2004) Journalist (G)
Highgate Cemetery (East), London

FORMBY, George (1904-1961) Entertainer (G)
Warrington Cemetery, Warrington

FOWLER, John (1817-1898) Civil/ Railway Engineer (G)
Brompton Cemetery, London

FRASER, Ronald (1930-1997) Actor (G)
  Hampstead Cemetery, London

FREUD, Lucian (1922-2011) Artist (G)
  Highgate Cemetery (West), London

FREUD, Sigmund (1856-1939) Founder of Psychoanalysis (M)
  Golders Green Crematorium, London

FURY, Billy (1940-1983) Singer (G)
  Mill Hill (Paddington New) Cemetery, London

GAINSBOROUGH, Thomas (1727-1788) Painter (G)
  St Anne's Church, Kew, London

GAITSKELL, Hugh (1906-1963) Labour Politician (G)
  St John at Hampstead, London

GEORGE V (1865-1936) British Monarch (G)
  St George's Chapel, Windsor, Berkshire

GEORGE VI (1895-1952) British Monarch (G)
  St George's Chapel, Winsdor, Berkshire

GEORGE, David Lloyd (1863-1945) Prime Minister (M)
  On banks of River Dwyfor, Llanystumdwy, Gwynedd

GIBBONS, Grinling (1648-1721) Sculptor/ wood carver (M)
  St Paul's Church, Covent Garden, London

GILBERT, W.S. (1836-1911) Dramatist, Librettist (G)
  Church of St John the Evangelist, Stanmore

GLOVER, Brian (1934-1997) Televison and Film Actor (G)
  Brompton Cemetery, London

GRADE, Lew (1906-1998) Media Mogul (G)
  Willesden United Synagogue Cemetery, London

GRAY, Henry (1827-1861) Surgeon, Author of Gray's Anatomy (G)
  Highgate Cemetery (West), Highgate, London

GRAYSON, Larry (1923-1995) Comedian, Presenter (G)
  Oaston Road Cemetery, Nuneaton, Warwickshire

GREEN, Hughie (1920-1997) T,V Personality (M)
  Golders Green Crematorium, London

ARTHUR TOWLE
1885 - 1954
ALSO KNOWN AS
ARTHUR LUCAN
OLD MOTHER RILEY

"Matches Penny A Box
Stop Me And Strike One,
I've Not Had A Box Of
Matches ... Months
My ... Getting

Arthur Lucan

IN LOVING
MEMORY OF
MEG
DAWSON
BELOVED WIFE
AND MOTHER
DIED 15TH APRIL 1986.
AGED 48 YEARS.
AND NOW GRANDMA

ALSO
LES
DAWSON
BELOVED HUSBAND
DAD AND GRANDAD
DIED 10TH JUNE 1993
AGED 62 YEARS.

"THEY WALKS IN
THE WARMTH OF
ETERNAL SUNSHINE
AND SLEEPS WHERE
NO SHADOWS FALL"
PEACE

Les Dawson

Mark Jones

Tommy Taylor

David Pegg

In
Affectionate Remembrance
of
BRIAN JONES
born 28th february 1942
died 3rd july 1969
at Hartfield. Sussex

Brian Jones

JOHN WISDEN
Born September 5 1826
Died April 5 1884
Sussex and All-England cricketer
Founder of Wisden Cricketers' Almanack

John Wisden

GRESLEY, Nigel (1876-1941) Locomotive Engineer (G)
St Peter Churchyard, Netherseal, Derbyshire

HALLEY, Edmond (1656-1742) Scientist (G)
St Margaret's Church, Lee, London

HANDEL, George Frederic (1685-1759) Classical Composer (G)
Westminster Abbey, London

HARRIS, Augustus (1825-1873) Actor, Theatrical Producer (G)
Brompton Cemetery, London

HAWKING, Stephen (1942-2018) Cosmologist (G)
Westminster Abbey

HARBEN, Philip (1906-1970) Television chef (G)
Highgate Cemetery (West), London

HARBIN, Robert (1908-1978) Magician (M)
Golders Green Crematorium, London

HARDING, Gilbert (1907-1960) T.V.Personality (G)
St Mary's R.C.Cemetery, Kensal Green, London

HARRISON, John (1693-1776) Inventor of Chronometer (G)
St John at Hampstead, London

HART, Tony (1925-2009) Artist, TV Presenter (G)
Christ Church Churchyard, Shamley Green, Waverley, Surrey

HARTLEY, Donna (1955-2013) Athlete (G)
Holy Trinity Churchyard, Wentworth, Rotherham

HATHAWAY, Anne (1556-1623) Wife of William Shakespeare (G)
Holy Trinity Church, Stratford upon Avon

HAY, Will (1888-1949) Comedy Actor (G)
Streatham Park Cemetery/ Crematorium

HAYES, Tubby (1935-1973) Jazz musician (M)
Golders Green Crematorium, London

HAYNES, Arthur (1914-1966) Comedian (G)
Hammersmith New Cemetery, London

HAYTER, George (1792-18710 Artist (G)
East Finchley Cemetery and Crematorium, East Finchley, London

HEARNE, Richard (1908-1979) Actor "Mr Pastry" (G)
St Mary the Virgin Churchyard, Platt, Kent

HEATH, Edward (1916-2005) Prime Minister (G)
Salisbury Cathedral

HENDERSON, Dickie (1922-1985) Entertainer
St Mary's R.C.Cemetery Kensal Green, London

HENDRY, Ian (1931-1984) Actor (M)
Golders Green Crematorium, London

HENRY V (1386-1422) English Monarch (G)
Westminster Abbey, London

HENRY VIII (1491-1547) English Monarch (G)
St George's Chapel, Windsor, Berkshire

HEPWORTH, Barbara (1903-1975) Sculptor (G)
Longstone Cemetery, Carbis Bay, St Ives, Cornwall

HERSCHEL, William (1738-1822) Astronomer (G)
St Laurence's Church, Upton, Slough

HILL, Benny (1924-1992) Comedian (G)
Hollybrook Cemetery, Shirley, Southampton, Hampshire

HILL, Rowland (1795-1879) Politician, established penny post (M)
Highgate Cemetery (West), London

HOLLIDAY, Michael (Norman Alexander Milne) (1924-1963) Singer (G)
Anfield Cemetery and Crematorium, Liverpool

HOLLOWAY, Stanley (1890-1982) Entertainer (G)
St Mary's the Virgin Church, East Preston, West Sussex

HOLST, Gustav (1874-1934) Classical Composer (G)
Chichester Cathedral, Chichester

HOWARD, Katherine (1523-1542) Fifth wife of Henry VIII (M)
Chapel of St Peter-ad-Vincula, Tower of London

HOWARD, Trevor (1913-1988) Actor (G)
St Peter Chuchyard, Arkley, Barnet, London

HOWERD, Frankie (1917-1992) Comedian (G)
St Gregory Churchyard, Weare, Somerset

HOGARTH, William (1697-1764) Artist (G)
   Chiswick Old Cemetery, Chiswick, London

HULL, Rod (1935-1999) Puppeteer
   Addlestone Cemetery, Runnymede, Surrey

HUNTSMAN, Benjamin (1704-1776) Inventor of Crucible Steel (G)
   Attercliffe Cemetery, Sheffield

JAMES, Sid (1913-1976) Comedy Actor (M)
   Golders Green Crematorium, London

JAFFA, Max (1911-1991) Musician (M)
   Golders Green Crematorium, London

JOHN (1167-1216) English Monarch (G)
   Worcester Cathedral, Worcester

JONES, Brian (1942-1969) Rolling Stones Band Member (G)
   Prestbury Cemetery, Cheltenham

JONES, Mark (1933-1958) Manchester United "Busby Babe" Footballer (G)
   Wombwell Cemetery, Barnsley

KATHERINE of ARAGON (1485-1536) First wife of Henry VIII (G)
   Peterborough Cathedral, Peterborough, Huntingdonshire

KELVIN, William Thomson (1824-1907) Scientist "Kelvin Scale" (G)
   Westminster Abbey, London

KENNEDY, Kathleen Agnes "Kick" (1920-1948) Sister of John F.Kennedy (G)
   St Peter's Churchyard, Edensor, Chatsworth, Derbyshire

KIPLING, Rudyard (1865-1936) Writer/ Poet (M)
   Westminster Abbey, London

KNUTT, Bobby (1945-2017) Comedian, Actor (G)
   Holy Trinity Churchyard, Wentworth, Rotherham

KUNZ, Charlie (1896-1958) Pianist and Bandleader (G)
   Streatham Park Cemetery, London

LA RUE, Danny (1927-2009) Entertainer (G)
   St Mary's R.C.Cemetery, Kensal Green, London

LE MESURIER, John (1912-1983) Actor (M)
   St George Le Martyr Churchyard, Ramsgate

LAING, John (1879-1978) John Laing and Son Building Contractors (G)
Mill Hill (Paddington New) Cemetery, London

LAMBERT, Constant (1905-1951) Composer and Conductor (G)
Brompton Cemetery, London

LAUDER, Harry (1870-1950) Singer and Comedian (G)
Bent Cemetery, Hamilton, Glasgow, Scotland

LE MESURIER, John (1912-1983) Actor (M)
St George's Churchyard, Ramsgate, Kent

LEIGH, Vivien (1913-1967) Actress
Ashes scattered on the lake at Tickerage Mill, Blackboys, Sussex

LENNON, Julia Stanley (1914-1958) Mother of John Lennon (G)
Allerton Cemetery, Liverpool

LENO, Dan (1860-1904) Music Hall Comedian (G)
Lambeth Cemetery London

LEVIN, Bernard (1928-2004) Author, Broadcaster (G)
Brompton Cemetery, London

LEYBOURNE, George (1842-1884) Music Hall Singer (G)
Abney Park Cemetery, Stoke Newington

LISTER, Anne (1791-1840) Gentleman Jack (G)
St John the Baptist Churchyard, Halifax

LISTER, Joseph (1827-1912) Medical Pioneer (G)
Hampstead Cemetery London

LITTLE JOHN, reputedly Robin Hood's right hand man (G)
St Michael's and All Angels Churchyard, Hathersage,
Derbyshire

LITTLE TICH (Harry Relph) (1869-1928) Music Hall Comedian (G)
East Finchley Cemetery, London

LITVINENKO, Alexander (1962-2006) Russian secret service (G)
Highgate Cemetery (West), London

LIVINGSTONE, David (1813-1873) Missionary (G)
Westminster Abbey, London

LLOYD GEORGE, David (1863-1945) British Prime Minister (G)
Llanystumdwy, Gwynedd, Wales

LLOYD, Marie (1870-1922) Music Hall Singer (G)
>> Hampstead Cemetery, London

LOBB, John (1829 -1895) Bespoke boot and shoe maker (G)
>> Highgate Cemetery (East), London

LOCKE, Joseph (1805-1860) Civil Engineer (G)
>> Kensal Green Cemetery London

LONGTHORNE, Joe (1955-2019) Singer (G)
>> Layton Cemetery, Blackpool

LOSS, Joe (1909-1990) Band Leader (G)
>> Bushey Jewish Cemetery London

LOWE, Arthur (1915-1982) Actor (M)
>> Sutton Coldfield Crematorium, Sutton Coldfield

LOWRY, Laurence Stephen (1887-1976) Artist (G)
>> Southern Cemetery, Chorlton-Cum-Hardy, Manchester

LUCAN, Arthur (1887-1954) Entertainer "Old Mother Riley" (G)
>> Eastern Cemetery, Hull

MACMILLAN, Harold (1894-1986) Prime Minister (G)
>> St Giles Churchyard, Horsted Keynes, West Sussex

MARX, Karl (1818-1883) Philosopher (G)
>> Highgate Cemetery (East), London

MARY STUART, "Queen of Scots" (1542-1587) Scottish Monarch (G)
>> Westminster Abbey, London

MASEFIELD, John Edward (1878-1967) English Poet Laureate (M)
>> Westminster Abbey, London

MATCHAM, Frank (1854-1920) Theatre Architect (G)
>> Highgate Cemetery (East), London

MATTHEWS, Jessie (1907-1981) Actress {M}
>> Breakspear Crematorium, Ruislip, London

MATTHEWS, Stanley (1915-2000) Footballer {M}
>> Ashes scattered at Britannia Stadium, Stoke

MARGARET, Princess (1930-2002) (M)
>> St George's Chapel, Windsor

MARPLES, Alfred Ernest (1907-1978) Politician (G)
    Southern Cemetery, Chorlton-Cum-Hardy, Manchester

MAYALL, Rik (1958-2014) Comedian, Actor
    Mayall Family Farm Grounds, East Allington, Totnes, Devon

MCGEE, Henry (1929-2006) Actor (G)
    Brompton Cemetery, London

MCLAREN, Malcolm (1946-2010) Impresario, clothes designer (G)
    Highgate Cemetery (East), London

MERCURY, Freddie (1946-1991) Singer.   Kensal Green Cemetery London
    (ashes scattered at Lake Lucerne Switzerland)

MICHAEL, George (1963-2016) Singer (G)
    Highgate Cemetery (West), London

MILLER, Max (1894-1963) Comedian (M)
    Downs Crematory, Brighton

MILLIGAN, Spike (1918-2002) Comedian/ Scriptwriter (G)
    Winchelsea Churchyard, Winchelsea, East Sussex

MILLS, John (1908-2005) Actor (G)
    Saint Mary the Virgin Churchyard, Denham, Buckinghamshire

MILLS, Freddie (1919-1965) Boxer (G)
    Camberwell New Cemetery and Crematorium, Camberwell,
    London

MILTON, John (1608-1674) Poet (G)
    St Giles' Cripplegate, London

MOON, Keith (1946-1978) Drummer (The Who) (M)
    Golders Green Crematorium, London

MOORE, Bobby (1941-1993) Footballer (M)
    City of London Cemetery and Crematorium, Newham, London

MOORE, Henry (1898-1986) Sculptor (G)
    St Pauls Cathedral, London

MONTGOMERY, James (1771-1854) Philanthropist/ Poet (G)
    Cemetery Road Cemetery, Sheffield

MORECAMBE, Eric (1926-1984) Comedian (M)
    St Nicholas Churchyard, Harpenden, Hertfordshire

MORRIS, Dave (1896-1960) Comedian (G)
Layton Cemetery, Blackpool

MORRIS, William (1834-1896) Fabric Designer etc (G)
Kelmscot Church, Kelmscot

NEAGLE, Anna (1904-1986) Actress (G)
City of London Cemetery and Crematorium, Newham

NELSON, Admiral Horatio (1758-1805) British Naval Admiral (G)
Westminster Abbey, London

NEWTON, Isaac (1642-1727) Scientist, Astronomer (G)
Westminster Abbey, London

NIGHTINGALE, Florence (1820-1910) Pioneer Nurse (G)
St Margaret of Antioch Churchyard, East Wellow, Hampshire

NOLAN, Bernadette (1960-2013) Singer (Nolan Sisters) (M)
Carleton Crematorium, Blackpool

NORTHCLIFFE, Lord (1865-1922) Founder of Daily Mail (G)
East Finchley Cemetery and Crematorium, London

NOVELLO, Ivor (1893-1951) Composer (G)
Golders Green Crematorium, London

OLDFIELD, Maurice (1915-1981) Chief of Special Intelligence Services (G)
Over Haddon, Bakewell, Derbyshire

OLIVIER, Laurence (1907-1989) Actor (M)
Westminster Abbey, London

ORWELL, George [Eric Arthur Blair] (1903-1950) Author (G)
All Saints Churchyard, Sutton Courtney, Oxfordshire.

OWEN, Bill (1914-1999) Actor (G)
St John the Evangelist Churchyard, Upperthong, Kirklees,
Huddersfield

PANKHURST, Emmeline (1852-1928) Suffragette Leader (G)
Brompton Cemetery, London

PARNELL, Val (1892-1972) Musician (M)
Golders Green Crematorium, London

PARR, Katherine (1512-1548) Sixth wife of Henry VIII (G)
St Marys Chapel, Sudeley Castle, Winchcombe, Gloucestershire

Patrick Caulfield

Brian Glover

John Ruskin

Samuel Sotheby

67

PARRY, Charles Hubert Hastings (1848-1918) Classical Composer (G)
St Pauls Cathedral, London

PATERSON, Jennifer (1928-1999) T.V.Celebrity Cook ("Two Fat Ladies") (M)
Putney Vale Cemetery and Crematorium, London

PAXTON, Joseph (1803-1865) Designer of "Crystal Palace" for 1851 Great
Exhibition (G) St Peter Churchyard, Edensor, Chatsworth,
Derbyshire

PEGG, David (1935-1958) Manchester United "Busby Babe" Footballer (G)
Redhouse Cemetery, Adwick-le-Street, Doncaster

PICKLES, Wilfred (1904-1978) Radio Presenter (G)
Southern Cemetery, Chorlton-Cum-Hardy, Manchester

PINTER, Harold (1930-2008) Playwright (G)
Kensal Green Cemetery, London

PLOMLEY, Roy (1914-1985) Author and Broadcaster (G)
Putney Vale Cemetery and Crematorium, London

PROFUMO, John (1915-2006) British Politician (G)
St Peter's Churchyard,Hersham, Surrey

PROOPS, Marjorie (1911-1996) Journalist (G)
Golders Green Jewish Cemetery London

PURCELL, Henry (1659-1695) Classical Composer (G)
Westminster Abbey, London

RANDLE, Frank (1901-1957) Comedian. (G)
Carleton Cemetery Blackpool

RATTIGAN, Terence (1911-1977) Playwright (G)
Kensal Green Cemetery, London

REDGRAVE, Corin (1939-2010) Actor (G)
Highgate Cemetery (East), London

RELPH, Harry {Little Tich} (1867-1928) Music hall entertainer (G)
East Finchley Cemetery and Crematorium, East Finchley, London

REYNOLDS, Bruce (1931-2013) Mastermind Great Train Robbery (G)
Highgate Cemetery (East), London

REYNOLDS, Joshua (1723-1792) Artist (G)
St Paul's Cathedral, London

RICHARDSON, Ralph (1902-1983) Actor (G)
Highgate Cemetery (East), London

ROBINSON, Heath (1872-1944) Artist and Cartoonist (G)
East Finchley Cemetery and Crematorium, London

ROLLS, Charles Stewart (1877-1910) Automotive Pioneer (G)
Llangattock-Vibon-Avel Church Cemetery, Monmouth

ROSA, Carl (1842-1889) Opera manager, launched opera company (G)
Highgate Cemetery (West), London

ROSENTHAL, Jack (1931-2004) Writer/scriptwriter (G)
Golders Green Jewish Cemetery, London

ROSSETTI, Dante Gabriel (1828-1882) Artist (G)
All Saints Churchyard, Birchington, Kent

ROYCE, Frederick Henry (1863-1933) Automotive Pioneer
Ashes in Urn at Rolls Royce Headquarters (now moved elsewhere)

RUSKIN, John (1819-1900) Writer
St Andrews Churchyard, Coniston, Lake District (G)

RUTHERFORD, Ernest (1871-1939) Physicist (M)
Westminster Abbey, London

RUTHERFORD, Margaret (1892-1972) Actress (G)
St James Churchyard, Gerrards Cross, Buckinghamshire

SARGENT, John Singer (1856-1925) Artist (G)
Brookwood Cemetery, Woking

SARGENT, Malcolm (1895-1967) Classical Conductor (G)
Stamford Cemetery, Stamford

SAVILE, Jimmy (1926-2011) Radio/ T.V Presenter
Woodlands Cemetery, Scarborough (now removed)

SAYERS, Dorothy Leigh (1893-1957) Author
St Anne Churchyard, Wardour Street, Soho, London
(ashes below tower)

SCOTT, George Gilbert (1811-1878) Architect (G)
Westminster Abbey, London

SCOTT, Ronnie (1927-1996) Jazz Musician (M)
Golders Green Crematorium, London

SCOTT, Walter (1771-1832) Author (G)
Dryburgh Abbey, Melrose, Scotland

SEACOLE, Mary (1805-1881) Nurse Crimean War (G)
St Mary R,C Cemetery, Kensal Green, London

SECOMBE, Harry (1921-2001) Singer, comedian (M)
Christ Church Churchyard, Shamley Green, Waverley, Surrey

SELLARS, Peter (1925-1980) Comedy actor (M)
Golders Green Crematorium, London

SEYMOUR, Jane (1509-1537) Third Wife of Henry VIII (G)
St George's Chapel, Windsor

SHAKESPEARE, William (1564-1616) Playwright (G)
Holy Trinity Church, Stratford upon Avon

SHANE, Paul (1940-1981) Comedian, Actor (G)
East Herringthorpe Cemetery, Rotherham

SHELLEY, Mary (1797-1851) Novelist (G)
St Peter's Churchyard, Bournemouth

SHELTON, Anne (1923-1994) Singer (G)
Camberwell Cemetery and Crematorium, London

SIDDAL, Lizzie (1829-1862) Artist, wife of Dante Gabriel Rossetti {G}
Highgate Cemetery (West), London

SILLITOE, Alan (1928-2010), Novelist {G}
Highgate Cemetery (East), London

SMITH, John (1938-1994) Politician (G)
Saint Orans Chapel Cemetery, Isle of Iona, Scotland

SOANE, John (1753-1837) Architect (G)
St Pancras Old Church Churchyard, London

SOTHEBY, Samuel (1805-1868) Auctioneer (G)
Brompton Cemetery, London

SPODE, Josiah (1733-1797) Pioneering potter (G)
St Peter and Vincula Churchyard, Stoke on Trent

SPRINGFIELD, Dusty (1939-1999) Singer (M)
St Mary the Virgin, Henley on Thames

SQUIRES, Dorothy (1915-1998) Singer and Entertainer (G)
Streatham Park Cemetery, Streatham, London

STAFF, Kathy (1928-2008) Actress (G)
Dunkinfield Cemetery and Crematorium, Dunkinfield, Manchester

STARR, Edwin (1942-2003) Singer, Musician (G)
Southern Cemetery, West Bridgford, Nottingham

STARR, Freddie (1943-2019) Comedian (G)
Prescott Parish Church, Liverpool

STEPHENSON, George (1781-1848) Civil and Mechanical Engineer (G)
Holy Trinity Church, Chesterfield

STEPHENSON, Robert (1803-1859) Civil engineer (G)
Westminster Abbey, London

STOKOWSKI, Leopold (1882-1977) Conductor (G)
East Finchley Cemetery and Crematorium, East Finchley, London

STUBBS, George (1724-1866) Artist (M)
East Finchley Cemetery and Crematorium, East Finchley, London

SULLIVAN, Arthur (1842-1900) Composer (G)
St Pauls Cathedral, London

SUTCLIFFE, Stuart (1940-1962) Original member of the Beatles (G)
Huyton Parish Church Cemetery,

TAFLER, Sidney (1916-1979) Actor (G)
Golders Green Jewish Cemetery, London

TAUBER, Richard (1891-1948) Operatic Tenor (G)
Brompton Cemetery, London

TAYLOR, Tommy (1932-1958) Manchester United "Busby Babe" Footballer
(G) Monk Bretton Cemetery, Barnsley

TELFORD, Thomas (1757-1834) Civil Engineer (G)
Westminster Abbey, London

TENNYSON, Alfred (1809-1892) Poet (G)
Westminster Abbey, London

THACKERAY, William (1811-1863) Novelist (G)
Kensal Green Cemetery, London

THATCHER, Margaret (1925-2013) Prime Minister (M)
Ashes scattered at Royal Hospital, Chelsea Burial Ground, London

THATCHER, Denis (1915-2003) (M)
Ashes scattered at Royal Hospital, Chelsea Burial Ground, London

TILLEY, Vesta (1864-1952) Actress/Music Hall Performer (G)
Putney Vale Cemetery and Crematorium, London

TODD, Richard (1919-2009) Actor (G)
St Guthlac's Churchyard, Little Ponton, Lincolnshire

TOLKEIN, J.R.R. (1892-1973) Author (G)
Wolvercote Cemetery, Oxford

TROLLOPE, Anthony (1815-1882) Author (G)
Kensal Green Cemetery, London

TURNER, Joseph Mallord William (1775-1851) Artist (G)
Saint Pauls Cathedral, London

TUSSAUD, Marie (1761-1850) Waxworks modeller (G)
St Mary's Catholic Church, Cadogan Street, London

VAUGHAN, Frankie (1928-1999) Singer (G)
Bushey Jewish Cemetery, London

VICTORIA, Queen (1819-1901) British Monarch (G)
Frogmore, Windsor

WALL, Max (1908-1990) Comedian and Entertainer (G)
Highgate Cemetery (East), London

WALTON, Isaac (1593-1683) Author (G)
Winchester Cathedral, Winchester

WARRISS, Ben (1909-1993) Comedian/Entertainer (G)
Streatham Park Cemetery, Streatham, London

WATERHOUSE, John William (1849-1917) Artist (G)
Kensal Green Cemetery, London

WATT, James (1736-1819) Inventor {G}
St Mary Churchyard, Handsworth, Birmingham

WEDGWOOD, Josiah (1730-1795) Pioneering potter (G)
St Peter and Vicula Churchyard, Stoke on Trent

WELLESLEY, Arthur (1769-1852) 1st Duke of Wellington (G)
St Paul's Cathedral, London

WESLEY, Charles (1707-1788) Religious composer (G)
East Finchley Cemetery and Crematorium, East Finchley, London

WESLEY, John (1703-1791) Theologian and Evangelist (G)
Wesley's Chapel, City Road, London

WHEATLEY, Dennis (1897-1977) Author (M)
Brookwood Cemetery, Woking

WINEHOUSE, Amy (1983-2011) Singer (G)
Edgwarebury Cemetery, Edgware, London

WHISTLER, James McNeill (1834-1903) Artist (G)
Chiswick Old Cemetery, Chiswick, London

WHITE, Carol (1943-1991) Actress (M)
Mortlake Cemetery, London

WILBERFORCE, William (1759-1833) Slavery abolitionist (G)
Westminster Abbey, London

WILLIAMS, Ralph Vaughan (1872-1958) Classical Composer (M)
Westminster Abbey, London

WILSON, Harold (1916-1995) Prime Minister (G)
St Mary Old Churchyard, St Marys, Isles of Scilly

WINTERS, Bernie (1933-1991) Comedian/Entertainer (M)
Golders Green Crematorium, London

WISDEN, John (1826-1884) Cricketer and Founder of Wisden's Almanack
(G) Brompton Cemetery, London

WISDOM, Norman (1915-2010) Actor/ comedian (G)
Kirk Bride, Bride, Isle of Man

WORDSWORTH, William (1770-1850) Poet (G)
St Oswald Churchyard, Grasmere, Cumbria

WORSLEY, Arthur (1920-2001) Ventriloquist. (G)
Carleton Cemetery, Blackpool

WREN, Christopher (1632-1723) Architect/Scientist/Astronomer (G)
St Pauls Cathedral, London

WRIGHT, Billy (1924-1994) Footballer
        Ashes scattered at Molineux Stadium,
        Wolverhampton

WYMARK, Patrick (1926-1970) Actor (G)
        Highgate Cemetery (West),
        London

ZOFFANY, Johannes (1733-1810),
        Artist (G)
        St Anne's Church, Kew, London

Edward Elgar

74

CEMETERIES WITH FAMOUS GRAVES AND MEMORIALS (UK)

NOTE: If the deceased has been cremated, the ashes could have been scattered or taken elsewhere

ABBEYS, CATHEDRALS, TOWER OF LONDON, WINDSOR etc

ALTHORP HOUSE - NORTHAMPTONSHIRE
Diana, Princess of Wales (1961-1997) Island in the Lake

CANTERBURY CATHEDRAL
Thomas Becket (1118-1170) Archbishop of Canterbury

CHICHESTER CATHEDRAL
Gustav Holst (1874-1934) Classical Composer

FROGMORE – WINDSOR
Edward VIII (1894-1972) British Monarch
Price Albert (1819-1861) English Royalty

Queen Victoria (1819-1901) British Monarch

MELROSE – SCOTLAND
DRYBURGH ABBEY
Walter Scott (1771-1832) Author

PETERBOROUGH CATHEDRAL
Katherine of Aragon (1485-1536) First wife of Henry VIII

SALISBURY CATHEDRAL
Edward Heath (1916-20050 Prime Minister

ST GEORGE'S CHAPEL – WINDSOR
Charles I (1600-1649) English Monarch
Edward VII (1841-1910) British Monarch
George V (1865-1936) British Monarch
George VI (1895-1952) British Monarch
Henry VIII (1491-1547) British Monarch
Princess Margaret (1930-2002) Sister of Queen Elizabeth II

Jane Seymour (1509-1537) Third wife of Henry VIII
Elizabeth Windsor (1900-2002) Mother of Queen Elizabeth II

ST PAULS CATHEDRAL

Alexander Fleming (1881-1955) Scientist
Henry Moore (1898-1986) Sculptor
Charles Parry (1848-1918) Classical composer
Joshua Reynolds (1723-1792) Painter
Arthur Sullivan (1842-1900) Composer
J.M.W.Turner (1775-1851) Painter
Arthur Wellesley (1769-1852) 1st Duke of Wellington
Christopher Wren (1632-1723) Architect/ Scientist/ Astronomer

ST PAULS CHURCH, COVENT GARDEN

Grinling Gibbins (1648-1721) Sculptor/ wood carver
Peter Lely (1618-1680) Painter/ artist

SUDELEY CASTLE

ST MARY'S CHAPEL
Katherine Parr (1512-1548) Sixth wife of Henry VIII

TOWER OF LONDON

Anne Boleyn (1501-1536) Second wife of Henry VIII
Katherine Howard (1523-1542) Fifth wife of Henry VIII

WESTMINSTER ABBEY

Robert Adam (1728-1792) Architect
Anne I (1665-1714) British Monarch
Anne of Cleves (1515-1557) Fourth wife of Henry VIII
Clement Attlee (1883-1967) British Prime Minister
William Sterndale Bennett (1816-1875) Classical Composer
Ernest Bevin (1881-1951) Politician
Robert Browning (1812-1889) Poet
Charles II (1630-1685) English Monarch
Geoffrey Chaucer (1342-1400) Author
Oliver Cromwell (1599-1658) English Statesman (original burial site)
Charles Darwin (1809-1882) Scientist, Naturalist
Charles Dickens (1812-1870) Author
Richard Dimbleby (1913-1965) TV Presenter
Edward III (1312-1377) English Monarch
Elizabeth I (1533-1603) English Monarch
Stephen Hawking (1942-2018) Cosmologist
George Frederick Handel (1685-1759) Composer
Henry V (1386-1422) English Monarch
William Thomsen Kelvin (1824-1907) Scientist "Kelvin Scale"

Rudyard Kipling (1865-1936) Author
David Livingstone (1813-1873) Missionary
Mary Stuart "Queen of Scots" (1542-1587) Scottish Monarch
John Edward Masefield (1878-1967) English Poet Laureate
Admiral Horatio Nelson (1758-1805) British Naval Admiral
Isaac Newton (1642-1727) Scientist, Astronomer
Laurence Olivier (1907-1989) Actor
Henry Purcell (1659-1695) Classical Composer
Ernest Rutherford (1871-1937) Physicist
George Gilbert Scott (1811-1878) Architect
Robert Stephenson (1803-1859) Civil Engineer
Thomas Telford (1757-1834) Civil Engineer
Alfred Tennyson (1809-1892) Poet
Ralph Vaughan Williams (1872-1958) Classical Composer
William Wilberforce (1759-1833) Slavery Abolitionist

WINCHESTER CATHEDRAL

Alfred the Great (849-899) Anglo Saxon Monarch
Jane Austen (1775-1817) Novelist
Canute (995-1035) English Monarch
Isaac Walton (1593-1683) Author

WORCESTER CATHEDRAL

John (1167-1216) British Monarch

LONDON and DISTRICT

ARKLEY – BARNET

ST PETER CHURCHYARD
Trevor Howard (1913-1988) Actor

ABNEY PARK CEMETERY – STOKE NEWINGTON
William Booth (1829-1912) Founder of Salvation Army
Albert Chevalier (1861-1923) Music Hall Singer/ Comedian
George Leybourne (1842-1884) Music Hall Singer

ALL SAINTS CHURCHYARD - CHELSEA
Hans Sloane (1660-1753) Benefactor of British Museum

BROMPTON CEMETERY
Charles Coborn (1852-1945) Music Hall Singer
Samuel Cunard (1787-1865) Founder of Cunard Line
John Fowler (1817-1898) Civil/ railway Engineer
Brian Glover (1934-1997) Television and film actor
Augustus Harris (1825-1873) Actor, theatrical producer
Constant Lambert (1905-1951) Composer and Conductor
Bernard Levin (1928-2004) Author, broadcaster
Henry McGee (1929-2006) Actor
Emmeline Pankhurst (1858-1928) Suffragette Leader
Samuel Sotheby (1805-1868) Auctioneer
Richard Tauber (1891-1948) Operatic Tenor
John Wisden (1826-1884) Founder of Wisden Almanack

BUNHILL FIELDS CITY ROAD
William Blake (1757-1827) Poet/Artist/Mystic
John Bunyan (1628-1688) Writer
Daniel Defoe (1661-1731) Author

BUSHEY JEWISH CEMETERY
Alma Cogan (1932-1966) Singer
Joe Loss (1909-1990) Band Leader
Frankie Vaughan (1928-1999) Singer

CAMBERWELL CEMETERY AND CREMATORIUM
Freddie Mills (1919-1965) Boxer
Anne Shelton (1923-1994) Singer

CHISWICK OLD CEMETERY
William Howgarth (1697-1764) Artist
James McNeill Whistler (1834-1903) Artist

CROYDON CEMETERY AND CREMATORIUM
Ronnie Corbett (1930-2016) Comedian

EAST FINCHLEY CEMETERY AND CREMATORIUM
Ainsworth, Alyn (1924-1990) Composer
Bentinck, William Henry Cavendish (1738-1809) Prime Minister
Harry Champion (1865-1942) Music Hall Singer
Robert Donat (1905-1958) Actor
George Hayter (1792-1871) Painter
Harry Relph (Little Tich) (1867-1928) Music Hall Entertainer
Lord Northcliffe (1865-1922) Founder of Daily Mail
Humphrey Lyttleton (1921-2008) Jazz Musician
Wendy Richard (1943-2009) Actress
Heath Robinson (1872-1944) Artist and Cartoonist
Leopold Stokowski (1882-1977) Classical Conductor
George Stubbs (1724-1866) Artist
Charles Wesley (1707-1788) Religious Music Composer
Kenneth Williams (1926-1988) Comic Actor

EDGWAREBURY CEMETERY
Winehouse, Amy (1983-2011) Singer

GOLDERS GREEN CREMATORIUM
(Ashes scattered or taken elsewhere)

Larry Adler (1914-200) Musician - Harmonica
Kingsley Amis (1922-1995) Author
Stanley Baldwin (1867-1947) Politician
Lionel Bart (1930-1999) Composer
Ernest Bevin (1881-1951) Politician
Enid Blyton (1898-1968) Author
Marc Bolan (1947-1977) Singer (T.Rex)
Bernard Bresslaw (1934-1993) Actor ("Carry-On" films)
Neville Chamberlain (1869-1940) Politician
Eric Coates (1886-1957) Composer
Ian Dury (1942-2000) Singer
T.S. Eliot (1888-1965) Poet
Ray Ellington (1916-1985) Jazz Musician
Kathleen Ferrier (1912-1953) Opera Singer
Bud Flanagan (1896-1968) Entertainer
Michael Foot (1913-2010) Politician
Sigmund Freud (1856-1939) Founder of Psychoanalysis
Erno Goldfinger (1902-1987) Architect
Denis Goodwin (1929-1975) Comedian, scriptwriter
Charles Gray (1928-2000) Actor
Benny Green (1927-1998) Jazz musician
Hughie Green (1920-1997) TV Personality
Joyce Grenfell (1910-1979) Actress/Comedienne

Irene Handl (1902-1987) Comedy actress
Tommy Handley (1892-1949) Comedian
Robert Harbin (1908-1978) Magician
Cedric Hardwick (1893-1964) Actor
Jack Hawkins (1910-1973) Actor
Tubby Hayes (1935-1973) Jazz Musician
Ian Hendry (1931-1984) Actor
Myra Hess (1890-1965) Pianist
Gerard Hoffnung (1925-1959) Humourist, musician
Kenneth Horne (1907-1969) Radio host
Jack Hylton (1892-1965) Band leader
John Inman (1935-2007) Actor
Max Jaffa (1911-1991) Musician
Sid James (1913-1976) Comedy actor
Jimmy Jewel (1909-1995) Comedian/ comedy actor
Terry Jones (1942-2020) Monty Python Comedy Team
Rudyard Kipling (1865-1936) Writer/ Poet
Charles Rennie Mackintosh (1868-1928) Architect
Matt Monro (1930-1985) Singer
Keith Moon (1946-1978) Drummer (The Who)
Ivor Novello (1893-1951) Composer
Joe Orton (1933-1967) Playwright
Val Parnell (1892-1972) Theatre Impressario
Ronnie Scott (1927-1996) Jazz Musician
Peter Sellers (1925-1980) Comedy actor
H.G. Wells (1866-1946) Author
Bernie Winters (1933-1991) Comedian

GOLDERS GREEN JEWISH CEMETERY
Jack Bruce (1943-2014) Musician
Jacqueline du Pre (1945-1987) Cellist
Marjorie Proops (1911-1996) Journalist
Jack Rosenthal (1931-2004) Writer/ scriptwriter
Sydney Tafler (1916-1979) Actor

HAMPSTEAD CEMETERY
Ronald Fraser (1930-1997) Actor
Joseph Lister (1827-1912) Medical Pioneer
Marie Lloyd (1870-1922) Music Hall Singer

HENLEY ON THAMES

ST MARY THE VIRGIN CHURCH
Dusty Springfield (1939-1999) Singer

HIGHGATE CEMETERY (East & West)
Douglas Adams (1952-2001) Writer, dramatist
Jacob Bronowski (1908-1974) Scientist and Broadcaster
Patrick Caulfield (1936-2005) Painter (Pop Art)

Charles Cruft (1852-1938) Founder of Dog Show
George Eliot (Mary Anne Evans) (1819-1880) Writer
Michael Faraday (1791-1867) Chemist and Physicist
Paul Foot (1937-2004) Journalist
Lucian Freud (1922-2011) Artist
Henry Gray (1827-1861) Surgeon, Author Gray's Anatomy
Philip Harben (1906-1970) Television Chef
Roland Hill (1795-1879) Politician, Established Penny Post
Alexander Litvinenko (1962-2006) Russian Secret Service
John Lobb (1829-1895) Bespoke Boot and Shoemaker
Karl Marx (1818-1883) Philosopher
Frank Matcham (1854-1920) Theatre Architect
Malcom McLaren (1946-2010) Impresario, Pop Artist
George Michael (1963-2016) Singer
Corin Redgrave (1939-2010) Actor
Bruce Reynolds (1932-2013) Mastermind of Great Train Robbery
Ralph Richardson (1902-1983) Actor
Carl Rosa (1842-1889) Opera Manager
Lizzie Siddal (1829-1862) Artist
Alan Sillitoe (1928-2010) Novelist
Max Wall (1908-1990) Comedian and Entertainer
Patrick Wymark (1926-1970) Actor

ISLINGTON

WESLEY'S CHAPEL
John Wesley (1703-1791) Theologian and Evangelist

KENSAL GREEN

KENSAL GREEN CEMETERY
Charles Babbage (1791-1871) Scientist/ Mathematician
Blondin (1824-1897) Tightrope Walker
Isambard Kingdom Brunel (1806-1859) Civil Engineer
Ossie Clark (1942-1996) Fashion Designer
Christine Keeler (1942-2017) Model
Joseph Locke (1805-1860) Civil Engineer
George Melly (1926-2007) Jazz Singer
Freddie Mercury (1946-1991) Popular Singer (cremated – ashes scattered at Lake Lucerne Switzerland)
Harold Pinter (1930-2008) Playwright
Terence Rattigan (1911-1977) Playwright
William Thackeray (1811-1863) Novelist
Anthony Trollope (1815-1882) Author
John William Waterhouse (1849-1917) Artist

ST MARY'S R.C. CEMETERY
John Barborolli (1899-1970) Orchestral Conductor

George Carmen (1929-2001) Barrister
Gilbert Harding (1907-1960) T.V Personality
Dickie Henderson (1922-1985) Entertainer
Danny La Rue (1927-2009) Actor, cabaret artist
Mary Seacole (1805-1881) Nurse Crimean War

KEW

ST ANNE'S CHURCH
Thomas Gainsborough (1727-1788) Painter
Johan Zoffany (1733-1810) Painter

LAMBETH

LAMBETH CEMETERY
Dan Leno (1860-1904) Music Hall Comedian

ST MARY CHURCHYARD
Elias Ashmole (1617-1692) Scientist

LEE

OLD ST MARGARET'S CHURCHYARD
Edmund Halley (1656-1742) Scientist, Astronomer

MILL HILL CEMETERY
Billy Fury (1940-1983) Singer
John Laing (1879-1978) John Laing and Sons Building Contractors

MORTLAKE CREMATORIUM
(Ashes scattered or taken elsewhere)

Richard Beckinsale (1947-1979) Actor
Tommy Cooper (1921-1984) Magician and Comedian
Dick Emery (1917-1983) Comedian
Kenny Everett (1944-1995) T.V and Radio Personality
Charles Hawtrey (1914-1988) Actor (Carry On series etc)
Teddy Johnson (1919-2018} Singer with Pearl Carr
Kirsty MacColl (1959-2000)   Singer
Stephen Thomas Ward (1912-1963) Osteopath (Profumo Affair)

MORTLAKE CEMETERY (AKA HAMMERSMITH NEW CEMETERY)
Arthur Haynes (1914-1966) Comedian
Carol White (1943-1991) Actress

NEWHAM

CITY OF LONDON CEMETERY AND CREMATORIUM
Bobby Moore (1941-1993) Footballer
Anna Neagle (1904-1986) Actress

OLD BROMPTON CEMETERY
Charles Coburn (1852-1945) Music Hall Singer
Samuel Cunard (1788-1865) Pioneer of Transatlantic Steam Navigation
Brian Glover (1934-1997) Actor
Emmeline Pankhurst (1858-1928) Leading Suffragette
John Wisden (1826-1884) Founder of Wisden Cricketers Almanac

OLD CHISWICK CEMETERY
William Hogarth (1697-1764) Painter
James McNeill Whistler (1834-1903) Artist

OLD MORTLAKE CEMETERY
Arthur Bliss (1891-1975) Classical Composer

PUTNEY VALE CEMETERY AND CREMATORIUM
(Ashes scattered or taken elsewhere)

Arthur Askey (1900-1982) Comedian
Stanley Baker (1927-1976) Actor and producer
Robert Beatty (1909-1992) Actor
James Beck (1929-1973) Actor (Dads Army)
Reginald Bosanquet (1932-1984) Newscaster
Howard Carter (1874-1939) Scientist/ Archeologist
Jacob Epstein (1880-1959) Sculptor (grave)
James Hunt (1947-1993) Racing Driver
Leonard Hutton (1916-1990) Cricketer
Hattie Jacques (1924-1980) Comedy Actress
James Laker (1922-1986) Cricketer
David Lean (1908-1991) Motion Picture Director
Kenneth More (1914-1982) Actor
Jennifer Paterson (1928-1999) One of the "Two Fat Ladies"
Jon Pertwee (1919-1996) Actor
Roy Plumley (1914-1985) Author and broadcaster
Nyree Dawn Porter (1940-2001) Actress
Joan Sims (1930-2001) Comedy Actress ("Carry On" films etc)
Vesta Tilley (1864-1952) Actress/Music Hall Performer (grave)

ROYAL HOSPITAL CHELSEA BURIAL GROUND
Margaret Thatcher (1925-2013) Prime Minister (ashes scattered)
Denis Thatcher (1915-2003) (ashes scattered)

RUISLIP

BREAKSPEAR CREMATORIUM
Pat Combs (1926-2002) Comedy Actress
Brian Connoly (1945-1997) Singer (The Sweet)
Kenneth Connor (1916-1993) Actor (Carry-On Series)
Dulcie Gray (1919-2011) Actress

Jessie Matthews (1907-1981) Actress
Peggy Mount (1915-2001) Actress

SHAMLEY GREEN - WAVERLEY

CHRIST CHURCH CHURCHYARD
Tony Hart (1925-2009) Artist and TV Presenter

SLOUGH

ST LAURENCE'S CHURCH, UPTON
William Herschel (1738-1822) Astronomer

SUNNINGDALE CATHOLIC CEMETERY
Diana Dors (1931-1984) Actress and Entertainer

ST ANNE CHURCHYARD, SOHO
Dorothy Leigh Sayers (1893-1957) Author

ST GILES' CRIPPLEGATE
John Milton (1608-1674) Poet

ST JOHN-AT–HAMPSTEAD
John Constable (1776-1837) Artist
Peter Cook (1937-1995) Satirist
Hugh Gaitskell (1906-1963) Labour Politician
John Harrison (1693-1776) Inventor of Chronometer

ST MARTIN-IN-THE-FIELDS CHURCH
Robert Boyle (1627-1691) Scientist

ST MARY'S R.C CHURCH, CHELSEA
Marie Tussaud (1761-1850) Waxworks Museum Founder

ST MARY'S R.C. CEMETERY HARROW
Dicky Henderson (1922-1985) Singer and comedian

ST PANCRAS OLD CHURCH CHURCHYARD
Johann Christian Bach (1735-1782) Classical Composer
John Soane (1753-1837) Architect
Mary Wollstonecraft (1759-1797) Writer, advocate of women's rights
(Her remains later removed to the Shelley family grave, Bournemouth)

STREATHAM

STREATHAM PARK CEMETERY/ CREMATORIUM
Graham Bond (1937-1974) Musician
Wilfred Bramwell (1912-1985) Actor
Desmond Decker (1942-2006) Reggae Musician
Gus Elen (1863-1940) Music Hall Singer/ Comedian

Will Hay (1888-1949) Comedy Actor
Charlie Kunz (1896-1958) Pianist and Bandleader
Donald McGill (1875-1962) Postcard Cartoonist
David Nixon (1919-1978) Magician
Dorothy Squires (1915-1998) Singer and Entertainer
Ben Warriss (1909-1993) Entertainer

TWICKENHAM

ST MARY'S CHURCHYARD
Alexander Pope (1688-1744) Poet
P.L Travers (1899-1996) Author

TWICKENHAM CEMETERY - WHITTON
Hylda Baker (1904-1986) Entertainer

WEST NORWOOD

WEST NORWOOD CEMETERY AND CREMATORIUM
Henry Bessemer (1813-1898) Inventor (Steel Industry)
Eric Morley (1918-2000) Entrepreneur
Henry Tate (1819-1899) Sugar Merchant

WILLESDEN UNITED SYNAGOGUE CEMETERY
Lew Grade (1906-1998) Media Mogul

WIMBLEDON

ST MARY'S CHURCHYARD
Joseph William Bazalgette (1819-1891) Victorian Engineer

PROVINCES

ADWICK-LE-STREET - DONCASTER

REDHOUSE CEMETERY
David Pegg (1935-1958) Manchester United "Busby Babe" Footballer

ALDEBURGH - SUFFOLK

ST PETER AND ST PAUL CHURCHYARD
Benjamin Britten (1913-1976) Classical Composer

BANBURY

BANBURY CREMATORIUM
Ronnie Barker (1929-2005) Actor/ Comedian

BARNSLEY

MONK BRETTON CEMETERY
Tommy Taylor (1932-1958) Manchester United "Busby Babe" Footballer

WOMBWELL CEMETERY
Mark Jones (1933-1958) Manchester United "Busby Babe" Footballer

CAWTHORNE, ALL SAINTS CHURCH
Ronnie Duke (- 1981) Entertainer (with Ricki Lee)

BEACONSFIELD

GREEN ACRES, CHILTERN
Peter Stringfellow (1940-2018) Impressario, Night Club Owner

BIRCHINGTON – KENT

ALL SAINTS CHURCHYARD
Dante Gabriel Rossetti (1828-1882) Artist

BIRMINGHAM

WITTON CEMETERY
John Cadbury (1801-1899) Chocolate Manufacturer

FRIENDS MEETING HOUSE BURIAL GROUND - BOURNVILLE
George Cadbury (1939-1922) Chocolate Maker

ST MARY CHURCHYARD, HANDSWORTH
James Watt (1736-1819) Mechanical Inventor

BLACKPOOL

CARLETON CEMETERY
Norman Evans (1901-1962) Variety, T.V and radio artist
Frank Randle (1901–1957) Comedian
Arthur Worsley (1920-2001) Ventriloquist

CARLETON CREMATORIUM
Lennie Bennett (1938-2009) Comedian
Charlie Cairoli (1910-1980) Clown and Musician
Violet Carson (1898-1983) Actress (Coronation Street)
Jimmy Clithero (1921-1973) Comedian
Reginald Dixon (1904-1985) Organist
Stanley Mortenson (1921-1991) Footballer
Bernadette Nolan (1960-2013) Singer (Nolan Sisters)
Beatrix Potter (1866-1943) Author

LAYTON CEMETERY
John Bickerstaffe (1848-1930) Chairman of Blackpool Tower
Joe Longthorne (1955-2019) Singer
Dave Morris (1896-1960) Comedian

LYTHAM PARK CEMETERY AND CREMATORIUM
Les Dawson (1931-1993) Comedian
Lynne Carol (1914-1990) Actress

BLAYDON - OXFORDSHIRE

ST MARTIN'S CHURCHYARD
Winston Churchill (1874-1965) Prime Minister

BOLTON

TONGE CEMETERY
Fred Dibnah (1938-2004) Steeplejack and TV Personality

BOURNEMOUTH

ST PETER'S CHURCHYARD
Mary Shelley (1797-1851) Novelist

BRADBOURNE – DERBYSHIRE

ST MARY'S CHURCHYARD
Alan Bates (1934-2003) Actor

BRIGHTON

DOWNS CREMATORY
Max Miller (1894-1963) Comedian
George Robey (1869-1954) Comedian/ Actor

BROAD CHALKE – WILTSHIRE

ALL SAINTS CHURCHYARD
Cecil Beaton (1904-1980) Photographer

CHATSWORTH - DERBYSHIRE

ST PETERS CHURCHYARD, ENDSOR
11th Duke of Devonshire (1920-2004)
Kathleen Kennedy (1920-1948) Sister of John F.Kennedy
Joseph Paxton (1803-1865) Gardener and Engineer

CHELTENHAM

PRESTBURY CEMETERY
Brian Jones (1942-1969) Rolling Stones band member

CHESTERFIELD

George Stephenson (1781-1848) Civil and Mechanical Engineer

CHIMSIDE - SCOTLAND

CHIMSIDE PARISH CHURCH CEMETERY
Jim Clark (1936-1968) Racing Driver

CHOLSEY – OXFORDSHIRE

ST MARY'S CHURCHYARD
Agatha Christie (1890-1976) Author

CONISTON – LAKE DISTRICT

ST ANDREWS CHURCHYARD
John Ruskin (1819-1900) Writer

CONISTON GRAVEYARD
Donald Campbell (1921-1967) Sportsman

CROMFORD – DERBYSHIRE

ST MARY CHURCHYARD
Richard Arkwright (1732-1792) Inventor

CROSS – SOMERSET

ST GREGORY CHURCHYARD
Frankie Howard (1917-1992)

DANEHILL – EAST SUSSEX

DANEHILL CEMETERY
Peter Butterworth (1919-1979) Actor ("Carry-On" films)
Janet Brown (1923-2011) Actress

DENHAM – BUCKINGHAMSHIRE

ST MARY THE VIRGIN CHURCHYARD
John Mills (1908-2005) Actor

EAST PRESTON – WEST SUSSEX

ST MARY'S THE VIRGIN
Stanley Holloway (1890-1982) Entertainer

EAST WELLOW – HAMPSHIRE

ST MARGARET OF ANTIOCH CHURCHYARD
Florence Nightingale (1820-1910) Pioneer Nurse

EASTBOURNE

EASTBOURNE CREMATORIUM
Malcolm Vaughan (1929-2010) Singer
Fanny Craddock (1909-1994) T.V Cook/ Celebrity (memorial)

FENSTANTON – CAMBRIDGESHIRE

ST PETER AND ST PAUL CHURCHYARD
Lancelot "Capability" Brown (1716-1783) Landscape Designer

GERRARDS CROSS - BUCKINGHAMSHIRE

ST JAMES CHURCHYARD
Margaret Rutherford (1892-1972) Actress

GLASGOW

BENT CEMETERY, HAMILTON
Harry Lauder (1870-1950) Singer and Comedian

GRASMERE - CUMBRIA

ST OSWALD'S CHURCHYARD
William Wordsworth (1770-1850) Poet

GREAT MISSENDEN – BUCKINGHAMSHIRE

St PETER AND St PAUL CHURCHYARD
Roald Dahl (1916-1990) Novelist

GREENOCK – SCOTLAND

GREENOCK CEMETERY
Abram Lyle (1820-1891) Sugar Refiner, Syrup Manufacturer

HALIFAX

ST JOHN THE BAPTIST CHURCHYARD
Anne Lister (1791-1840) Gentleman Jack

HARPENDEN - HERTFORDSHIRE

ST NICHOLAS CHURCHYARD
Eric Morecambe (1926-1984) Comedian

HATHERSAGE – DERBYSHIRE

ST MICHAEL AND ALL ANGELS CHURCHYARD
Little John – reputedly Robin Hood's right hand man

HAWORTH – YORKSHIRE

ST MICHAEL AND ALL ANGELS CHURCHYARD
Charlotte Bronte (1816-1855) Novelist

HERSHAM – SURREY

ST PETER'S CHURCHYARD
John Profumo (1915-2006) British Politician

HORSTED KEYNES – WEST SUSSEX

ST GILES CHURCHYARD
Harold Macmillan (1894-1986) Prime Minister

HUCKNALL – NOTTINGHAMSHIRE

ST MARY MAGDALENE CHURCH
Lord Byron (1788-1824) Author, Poet

HULL

EASTERN CEMETERY
Arthur Lucan (1887-1954) Entertainer {Old Mother Riley}

ISLE OF IONA - SCOTLAND

SAINT ORANS CHAPEL CEMETERY
Duncan I (1001-1040) Scottish Monarch
Macbeth (1005-1057) Scottish Monarch
Malcolm I (897-954) Scottish Monarch
John Smith (1938-1994) Politician

ISLE OF MAN

KIRK BRIDE, BRIDE
Norman Wisdom (1915-2010) Actor, Comedian

ISLES OF SCILLY

ST MARY OLD CHURCHYARD, ST MARY'S
Harold Wilson (1916-1995) Prime Minister

KELMSCOT

KELMSCOT CHURCH
William Morris (1834-1896) Fabric Designer etc

LIMPSFIELD

ST PETERS CHURCHYARD
Frederick Delius (1862-1934) Classical Composer
Sir Thomas Beecham (1879-1961) Classical Orchestra Conductor

LITTLE MALVERN

ST WULSTANS CHURCH
Edward Elgar (1857-1934) Classical Composer

LITTLE PONTON – LINCOLNSHIRE

ST GUTHLAC'S CHURCHYARD
Richard Todd (1919-2009) Actor

LIVERPOOL

ALLERTON CEMETERY
Cilla Black (1943-2015) Singer
Julia Stanley Lennon (1914-1958) Mother of John Lennon
Ken Dodd (1927-2018) Comedian

ANFIELD CEMETERY AND CREMATORIUM
Michael Holliday (1924-1963) Singer
Bill Shankly (1913-1981) Manager Liverpool Football Club

HUYTON PARISH CHURCH CEMETERY
Stuart Sutcliffe (1940-1962) Original member of the Beatles

KIRKDALE JEWISH CEMETERY
Brian Epstein (1934-1967) The Beatles Manager

PRESCOTT PARISH CHURCH
Freddie Starr (1943-2019) Comedian

LLANYSTUMDWY – GWYNEDD

David Lloyd George (1863-1945) British Prime Minister

MALDEN – ESSEX

MALDEN CEMETERY
Peter Brough (1916-1999) Ventriloquist

MANCHESTER

SOUTHERN CEMETERY, CHORLTON CUM HARDY
John Alcock (1892-1919) First non-stop transatlantic flight crossing
Matt Busby (1909-1994) Manchester United Football Manager
L.S.Lowry (1887-1976) Artist
Alfred Ernest Marples (1907-1978) Politician
Wilfred Pickles (1904-1978) Actor, Radio Presenter

DUNKINFIELD CEMETERY AND CREMATORIUM
Kathy Staff (1928-2008) Actress

MINSTEAD – HAMPSHIRE

ALL SAINTS CHURCHYARD
Arthur Conan Doyle (1859-1930) Author

MONMOUTH

LLANGATTOCK-VIBON-AVEL CHURCH CEMETERY
Charles Stewart Rolls (1877-1910) Automotive Pioneer

NETHERSEAL – DERBYSHIRE

ST PETER CHURCHYARD
Nigel Gresley (1876-1941) Locomotive Engineer

NOTTINGHAM

SOUTHERN CEMETERY, WEST BRIDGFORD
Edwin Starr (1942-2003) Singer, Musician

NUNEATON

OASTON ROAD CEMETERY
Larry Grayson (1923-1995) Comedian, Presenter

OVER HADDON - BAKEWELL, DERBYSHIRE

ST ANNE'S CHURCHYARD
Maurice Oldfield (1915-1981) Chief of Special Intelligence Services "C" MI6

OXFORD

WOLVERCOTE CEMETERY
J.R.R.Tolkein (1892-1973) Author

PENHURST – EAST SUSSEX

ST MICHAEL THE ARCHANGEL CEMETERY
Harry H. Corbett (1925-1982) Actor

PLATT – KENT

ST MARY THE VIRGIN CHURCHYARD
Richard Hearne (1908-1979) Actor (Mr Pastry)

PLYMOUTH

EFFORD CREMATORIUM
Harry Brearley (1871-1948) Inventor of stainless steel

PUBLOW – SOMERSET

ALL SAINTS CHURCHYARD
Acker Bilk (1929-2014) Musician

RAMSGATE

ST GEORGE LE MARTYR CHURCHYARD
John Le Mesurier (1912-1983) Actor

RUSHOCK – WORCESTERSHIRE

ST MICHAEL CHURCHYARD
John Bonham (1948-1980) Rock Musician (Led Zepplin)

ROTHERHAM

EAST HERRINGTHORPE CEMETERY
Paul Shane (1940-2013) Comedian, Actor

HOLY TRINITY CHURCH, WENTWORTH
Bobby Knutt (1945-2017) Comedian, Actor
Donna Hartley (1955-2013) Athlete

ROTHERHAM CREMATORIUM
Tony Capstick (1944-2003) Actor
Barry Elliott (1944-2018) One of the Chuckle Brothers
Lynne Perrie (1931-2006) Actress

SCARBOROUGH

DEAN ROAD CEMETERY
Henry Vandyke Carter (1831-1897) Surgeon, Anatomical Artist

ST MARY CHURCHYARD
Anne Bronte (1820-1849) Novelist

WOODLANDS CEMETERY
Jimmy Savile (1926-2011) Radio/ T.V Presenter (grave removed)

SEVENHAMPTON, GLOUCESTERSHIRE

ST ANDREW CHURCHYARD
Ian Fleming (1908-1964) Author

SHEFFIELD

ATTERCLIFFE CEMETERY
Benjamin Huntsman (1704-1776) Inventor of Crucible Steel

CROOKES CEMETERY
Henry Boot (1851-1931) Builder (Henry Boot Group)

GENERAL CEMETERY, CEMETERY ROAD
George Bassett (1818-1886) Founder of Liquorice Allsorts
Mark Firth (1819-1880) Steel Manufacturer
James Montgomery (1771-1854) Philanthropist/ Poet

NORTON CHURCHYARD
Francis Chantrey (1782-1841) Sculptor

SHIRLEY – HAMPSHIRE

HOLLYBROOK CEMETERY
Benny Hill (1924-1992) Comedian

SUTTON COLDFIELD

SUTTON COLDFIELD CREMATORIUM
Arthur Lowe (1915-1982) Actor

SUTTON COURTNEY – OXFORDSHIRE

ALL SAINTS CHURCHYARD
George Orwell (1903-1950) Author

ST ALBANS

ST MICHAEL'S CHURCHYARD
Francis Bacon (1561-1626) Philosopher

ST JOHN – JERSEY

ST JOHN'S CHURCH
Billy Butlin (1899-1980) Holiday Camp Entrepreneur

ST IVES – CORNWALL

LONGSTONE CEMETERY, CARBIS BAY
Barbara Hepworth (1903-1975) Sculptor

STAMFORD

STAMFORD CEMETERY
Sir Malcolm Sargent (1895-1967) Classical Conductor

STANMORE

CHURCH OF St JOHN THE EVANGELIST
W.S.Gilbert (1836-1911) Dramatist, Librettist

STOKE ON TRENT

ST PETER AND VINCULA CHURCHYARD
Josiah Spode (1733-1797) Pottery Pioneer
Josiah Wedgwood (1730-1795) Pottery Pioneer

STRATFORD UPON AVON

HOLY TRINITY CHURCH
William Shakespeare (1564-1616) Playwright
Anne Hathaway (1556-1623) Wife of William Shakespeare

TILLINGTON , PETWORTH – WEST SUSSEX

ALL HALLOWES CHURCHYARD
June Whitfield (1925-2018) Comedy actress

TREBETHERICK – CORNWALL

ST ENODOC CHUTCHYARD
John Betjeman (1906-1984) Poet

TRENT – DORSET

ST ANDREW CHURCHYARD
Geoffrey Fisher (1887-1972) Archbishop

UPPERTHONG, KIRKLEES – HUDDERSFIELD

ST JOHN THE EVANGELIST CHURCHYARD
Bill Owen (1914-1999) Actor

WARRINGTON

WARRINGTON CEMETERY
George Formby (1904-1961) Entertainer

WAVERLEY – SURREY

CHRIST CHURCH CHURCHYARD, SHAMLEY GREEN
Tony Hart (1925-2009) Artist, TV Presenter
Harry Secombe (1921-2001) Singer, Comedian

WEARE – SOMERSET

ST GREGORY CHURCHYARD
Frankie Howerd (1917-1992) Comedian

WESTON SUPER MARE

EBDON ROAD CEMETERY AND CREMATORIUM
Jill Dando (1961-1999) Journalist, TV Presenter

WHITCHURCH CANONICORUM - DORSET

CHURCH OF CANDIDA AND HOLY CROSS
Robin Day (1923-2000) Broadcaster

WINCHELSEA – EAST SUSSEX

WINCHELSEA CHURCHYARD
Spike Milligan (1918-2002) Comedian, Scriptwriter

WOKING

BROOKWOOD CEMETERY
Dodi Fayed (1955-1997) Motion Picture Producer (removed later)
John Singer Sargent (1856-1925) Artist
Dennis Wheatley (1897-1977) Author

YAXLEY – SUFFOLK

ST MARY THE VIRGIN CHURCHYARD
Frederick Ashton (1904-1988) Ballet Choreographer

CEMETERIES WITH FAMOUS GRAVES AND MEMORIALS (WORLDWIDE)

AMERICA (USA)

ALABAMHA – HUNTSVILLE

OAKWOOD MEMORIAL GARDENS
Little Richard (1932-2020) Singer

CALIFORNIA - CATHEDRAL CITY – RIVERSIDE COUNTY

DESERT MEMORIAL PARK, PALM SPRINGS
Busby Berkeley (1895-1976) Director, Choreographer Film Musicals
Sonny Bono (1935-1998) Singer, Politician
Betty Hutton (1921-2007) Actress
Frederick Loewe (1901-1988) Composer
Patrick Macnee (1922-2015) Actor
William Powell (1892-1984) Actor
Frank Sinatra (1915-1998) Singer, Actor, Entertainer

CALIFORNIA - LOS ANGELES

FOREST LAWN MEMORIAL PARK (HOLLYWOOD HILLS) L.A
Gene Autry (1907-1998) Actor, Singer
Lucille Desiree Ball (1911-1989) Comedy Actress (original burial site)
David Carradine (1936-2009) Actor "Kung Fu"
Bette Davis (1908-1989) Actress
Sandra Dee (1942-2005) Actress
Andy Gibb (1958-1988) Singer
Gabby (George) Hayes (1885-1969) American Motion Picture Actor
Buster Keaton (1895-1966) Motion Picture Comedy Actor
Dorothy Lamour (1914-1996) Actress "Road to…." Films
Charles Laughton (1899-1962) Actor
Stan Laurel (1890-1965) Comedy Actor "Laurel and Hardy"
Liberace (Wladziv Valentino) (1919-1987) Pianist
Rick Nelson (1940-1985) Singer
Lou Rawls (1933-2006) Singer
Telly Aristotle Savalas (1922-1994) Actor "Kojak"
Rod Steiger (1925-2002) Film and T.V. Actor

FOREST LAWN MEMORIAL PARK (GLENDALE) L.A
Gracie Allan (1902-1964) Comedienne, Actress
Humphrey DeForest Bogart (1899-1957) Actor

Betty Davis

Nat King Cole

Errol Flynn

Debbie Reynolds / Carrie Fisher

Buster Keaton

98

William Boyd (1895-1972) Actor "Hopalong Cassidy"
George Burns (1896-1996) Comedian, Actor
Nat King Cole (1919-1965) Singer. Pianist
Sam Cooke (1931-1964) Singer (Gospel, soul, blues)
Sammy Davis Junior (1925-1990) Entertainer
Walt Disney (1901-1966) Cartoon Film Pioneer
W.C. Fields (William Claude Dukenfield) (1880-1946) Comedian
Errol Flynn (1909-1959) Film Actor
Clark Gable (1901-1960) Film Actor
Samuel Goldwyn (1879-1974) Hollywood Producer/ Mogul
Jean Harlow (1911-1937) Actress
Michael Jackson (1958-2009) Singer/ Entertainer
Alan Ladd (1913-1964) Film Actor
Harold Lloyd (1893-1971) Comedy Film Actor
Carole Lombard (1908-1942) Actress
Chico Marx (1887-1961) Stage and Motion Picture Actor "Marx Brothers"
Tom Mix (1880-1940) Cowboy Actor
Clayton Moore (1914-1999) Actor "The Lone Ranger"
Mary Pickard (1892-1979) Actress
Red Skelton (1913-1997) Actor, Comedian
James (Jimmy) Stewart (1908-1997) Actor
Elizabeth Taylor (1932 -2011) Actress
Spencer Tracey (1900-1967) Actor

HILLSIDE MEMORIAL PARK, CULVER CITY L.A
Jack Benny (1894-1974) Actor, comedian
Eddie Cantor (1892-1964) Actor, Singer, Comedian
Cyd Charisse (1922-2008) Actress, Dancer
Max Factor (1877-1938) Cosmetics Magnate
Friz Freleng (1906-1995) Cartoon Animator
Eydie Gorme (1928-2013) Singer
Moe Howard (1897-1975) Comedy Actor (3 Stooges)
Al Johnson (1886-1950) Actor and Singer
Leonard Nimoy (1931-2015) Actor
Aaron Spelling (1923-2000) T.V Producer
Shelley Winters (1920-2006) Actress

HOLLYWOOD FOREVER CEMETERY L.A
Mel Blanc (1908-1989) Voice Actor (particularly cartoons)
Cecil B. De Mille (1881-1959) Movie Producer/ Director
Nelson Eddy (1901-1967) Singer and Actor
Douglas Fairbanks Junior (1909-2000) Actor
Peter Finch (1912-1977) Actor
Judy Garland (1922-1969) Singer, Actress
John Huston (1906-1987) Movie Director
Peter Lorre (1904-1964) Character Actor
Tyrone Power (1914-1958) Actor
Nelson Riddle (1921-1985) Composer/ Musician

Mickey Rooney (1920-20140 Actor
Carl Switzer "Alfalfa" (1927-1959) Actor "Our Gang"
Rudolph Valentino (1895-1926) Film Actor

HOLY CROSS CEMETERY - CULVER CITY L.A
Jackie Coogan (1914-1984) Silent Movie Actor
Bing Crosby (Harry Lillis) (1904-1977) Singer, Actor
Jimmy Durante (1893-1980) Comedian, Actor
Rita Hayworth (1918-1987) Actress
Mario Lanza (1921-1959) Classical and Modern Singer
Sharon Marie Tate (1943-1969) Actress/ Manson Victim
Al Martino (1927-2009) Singer
Mack Sennett (1880-1960) Silent Film Director/Producer

HOME OF PEACE MEMORIAL PARK EAST L.A
Curly Howard (1903-1952) Comedy actor (3 Stooges)
Louis B. Mayer (1885-1957) Motion Picture Executive
Jack Warner (1892-1978) Motion Picture Executive

INGLEWOOD PARK CEMETERY
Ray Charles (1930-2004) Singer/ Entertainer
Ella Fitzgerald (1918-1996) Jazz Singer
Betty Grable (1916-1973) Actress
Gypsy Rose Lee (1914-1970) Actress and Burlesque Stripper
Billy Preston (1946-2006) Soul Musician
Sugar Ray Robinson (1920-1989) Boxer

MISSION SAN FERNANDO REY DE ESPANA CEMETERY (MISSION HILLS)
Bob Hope (1903-2003) Comedian, Actor, Entertainer

OAKWOOD MEMORIAL PARK (CHATSWORTH)
Fred Astaire (1899-1987) Actor, Entertainer
Ginger Rogers (1911-1995) Actress, Singer, Dancer

PIERCE BROTHERS VALLEY OAKS MEMORIAL PARK
Karen Carpenter (1950-1983) Singer
Virginia Mayo (1920-2005) Film Actress
Harry Nilsson (1941-1994) Singer, Songwriter
Artie Shaw (1910-2004) Musician

PIERCE BROTHERS VALHALLA MEMORIAL PARK
Oliver Hardy (1892-1957) Comedy Actor "Laurel and Hardy"

WESTWOOD MEMORIAL PARK L.A
Jim Backus (1913-1989) Actor. Voice of "Mr Magoo"
James Coburn (1928-2002) Actor
Kirk Douglas (1916-2020) Actor

Farrah Fawcett (1947-2009) Actress
Eva Gabor (1919-1995) Actress
Burt Lancaster (1913-1994) Film Actor
Peggy Lee (1920-2002) Singer
Jack Lemmon (1925-2001) Actor
Dean Martin (1917-1995) Singer
Walter Matthau (1920-2000) Actor
Marilyn Monroe (1926-1962) Film Actress
Roy Orbison (1936-1988) Singer
Buddy Rich (1917-1987) Jazz Drummer
Mel Torme (1925-1999) Jazz Singer/ Actor
Billy Wilder (1906-2002) Writer/ Director/ Producer
Carl Wilson (1946-1998) Singer "Beach Boys"
Natalie Wood (1938-1981) Film Actress

CALIFORNIA - OAKLAND, ALAMEDA COUNTY

CHAPEL OF THE CHIMES COLUMBARIUM AND MAUSOLEUM
John Lee Hooker (1917-2001) Blues Singer

CALIFORNIA – PALO ALTO

ALTA MESA MEMORIAL PARK
Steve Jobs (1955-2011) Apple Business Magnate

COLORADO - CRAWFORD

GARDEN OF MEMORIES CEMETERY
Joe Cocker (1944-2014) Singer

CONNECTICUT

PUTNAM CEMETERY – GREENWICH
Victor Borge (1909-2000) Pianist, Coedian

CEDAR HILL CEMETERY - HARTFORD
Katherine Hepburn (1907-2003) Actress

DELAWARE

OLD FELLOWS CEMETERY - CAMDEN
Robert Mitchum (1917-1997) Actor

GEORGIA – ATLANTA

OAKLAND CEMETERY
Margaret Mitchell (1900-1949) Author

ILLINOIS - CHICAGO – EVERGREEN PARK

ST MARY'S CEMETERY
Little Walter {Marion Walter Jacobs} (1930-1968) R&B Singer

ILLINOIS - HILLSIDE – COOK COUNTY

OAKRIDGE-GLEN OAK CEMETERY
Howling Wolf (Chester Burnett) (1910-1976) Blues Singer/ Musician

ILLINOIS - SKOKIE, COOK COUNTY

MEMORIAL PARK AND CREMATORIUM
James Lewis Kraft (1874-1953) Industrialist, Kraft Foods
Elaine Stritch (1925-2014) Actress, singer

ILLINOIS - SPRINGFIELD

OAK RIDGE CEMETERY
Abraham Lincoln (1809-1865) President of U.S.A

ILLINOIS - WORTH, COOK COUNTY

RESTVALE CEMETERY
Muddy Waters (MckInley Morganfield) (1915-1983) Blues Singer

KENTUCKY - FRANKFORT

FRANKFORT CEMETERY
Daniel Boone (1734-1820) Frontiersman

KENTUCKY – LOUISVILLE

CAVE HILL CEMETERY
Colonel Sanders (1890-1980) Businessman
Muhammed Ali (1942-2016) Boxer

LOUISIANA – METAIRIE

PROVIDENCE MEMORIAL PARK & MAUSOLEUM
Fats Domino (1928-2017)

MARYLAND - BALTIMORE

WESTMINSTER BURIAL GROUND
Edgar Allan Poe (1809-1849) Author

MICHIGAN – DETROIT

FORD CEMETERY
Henry Ford (1863-1947) Industrialist

WOODLAWN CEMETERY
Aretha Franklin (1942-2018) Singer

MINNESOTA - CHANHASSEN CARVER COUNTY

PAISLEY PARK STUDIOS
Prince (1958-2016) Singer

MISSISSIPPI - QUITO, LEFLORE COUNTY

PAYNE CHAPEL MEMORIAL BAPTIST CHURCH
Robert Johnson (1911-1938) Blues Singer

MISSOURI - BRANSON

OZARKS MEMORIAL PARK
Andy Williams (1927-1912) Singer

MISSOURI – KANSAS CITY

LINCOLN CEMETERY
Charlie "Bird" Parker (1920-1955) Jazz Musician

NEBRASKA – LINCOLN

WYUKA CEMETERY
Gordon MacRea (1921-1986) Actor, Singer

NEW JERSEY

FAIRVIEW CEMETERY, WESTFIELD
Witney Houston (1963-2012) Singer

NEW YORK

CYPRESS HILLS CEMETERY, BROOKLYN
Mae West (1893-1980) Actress
Piet Mondrian (1872-1944) Artist

FLUSHING CEMETERY, FLUSHING, QUEENS COUNTY
Louis Armstrong (1901-1971) Jazz singer
Dizzy Gillespie (1917-1993) Jazz musician

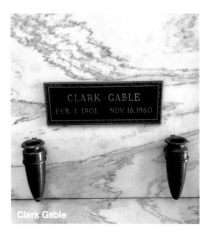

Clark Gable

Frank Sinatra

Walt Disney

Wyatt Earp

Marilyn Monroe

SAINT RAYMONDES CEMETERY, BRONX
Billie Holiday (1915-1959) Jazz singer

WOODLAWN CEMETERY, BRONX
Duke Ellington (1899-1974) Jazz musician

NEW YORK STATE - HARTSDALE – WESTCHESTER COUNTY

FERNCLIFF CEMETERY AND MAUSOLEUM
Bela Bartok (1881-1945) Classical composer
Joan Crawford (1985-1977) Actress
Judy Garland (1922-1969) Singer
Oscar Hammerstein II (1895-1960) Musical Lyricist
Jerome Kern (1885-1945) Composer
Alan Jay Lerner (1918-1986) Lyricist
Thelonious Monk (1917-1982) Jazz pianist, composer
Basil Rathbone (1892-1967) Actor
Paul Robeson (1898-1976) Singer
Sigmund Romburg (1887-1951) Composer
Ed Sullivan (1901-1974) Variety show host
Malcolm X (1925-1965) Social reformer, civil rights leader

NEW YORK STATE – NYACK - ROCKLAND COUNTY

OAKHILL CEMETERY,
Hopper, Edward, (1882-1967) Artist

NEW YORK STATE - VALHALLA – WESTCHESTER COUNTY

KENSICO CEMETERY
Ann Bancroft (1931-2005) Actress
Danny Kaye (1911-1987) Actor
Sergei Vasilievitch Rachmaninov (1973-1943) Classical Composer

NEVADA - LAS VEGAS

PALM MEMORIAL PARK
Tony Curtis (1925-2010) Actor

OHIO - CLEVELAND HEIGHTS

MAYFIELD CEMETERY
Paul Newman (1925-2008) Actor

TENNESSEE - HENDERSONVILLE

HENDERSONVILLE MEMORY GARDENS
Johnny Cash (1932-2003) Country singer

CEMETERIES WITH FAMOUS GRAVES AND MEMORIALS (WORLDWIDE)

TENNESSEE - MEMPHIS

GRACELAND MANSION ESTATES
Elvis Presley (1935-1977) Rock Singer, Actor

TEXAS - LUBBOCK

CITY OF LUBBOCK CEMETERY
Buddy Holly (1936-1959) Singer

VIRGINIA - ARLINGTON

ARLINGTON NATIONAL CEMETERY
John Glen (1921-2016) Astronaut
John. F. Kennedy (1917-1963) 35th United States President
Robert Kennedy (1925-1968) U.S Senator
Audie Murphy (1924-1971) Soldier, Actor
Jacqueline Kennedy Onasis (1929-1994) First Lady

VIRGINIA - MOUNT VERNON

MOUNT VERNON ESTATE
George Washington (1732-1799) 1st U.S President

WASHINGTON D.C

CONGRESSIONAL CEMETERY
John Philip Sousa (1854-1932) Composer

WASHINGTON - RENTON, KINGS COUNTY

GREENWOOD MEMORIAL PARK
Jimi Hendrix (1942-1970) Guitar Legend

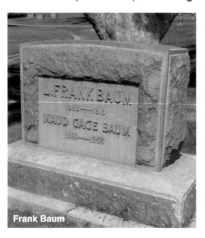
Frank Baum

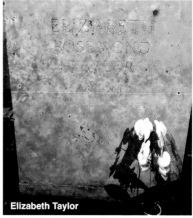
Elizabeth Taylor

AUSTRALIA

NORTH RYDE - NEW SOUTH WALES

NORTHERN SUBURBS CREMATORIUM
Michael Hutchence (1960-1997) Singer

AUSTRIA

EISENSTADT

EISENSTADT BURGENLAND
Joseph Haydn (1732-1809) Composer

VIENNA

CENTRAL CEMETERY
Ludwig Van Beethoven (1770-1827) Classical Composer
Willi Boskovsky (1909-1991) Classical Orchestra Conductor
Johannes Brahms (1833-1897) Classical Composer
Franz Schubert (1797-1828) Classical Composer
Johann Strauss I (1804-1849) Classical Composer
Johann Strauss II (1825-1899) Classical Composer
Franz von Suppe (1819-1895) Classical Composer

GRINZINGER CEMETERY
Gustav Mahler (1860-1911) Classical Composer

ST MARX CEMETERY
Wolfgang Amadeus Mozart (1756-1791) Classical Composer

KAPUZINERGRUFT
Habsburg I, Franz Joseph (1830-1916) Austrian Monarch
Josef I (1678-1711) Austrian Monarch
Josef II (1741-1790) Austrian Monarch
Plus many more Habsburg's in this crypt

CARIBBEAN

ST BARTHELEMY

LOW LORIENT CEMETERY
Johnny Halliday (1943-2017) French Singer

CYPRUS

KYKKOS

Jacques Offenbach

Edgar Degas

Adolphe Sax

Emile Zola

Rudolf Nureyev

THRONI MOUNTAIN TOMB
Archbishop Makarios lll (1913-1977) Guerrilla Leader

FRANCE

AIX-EN PROVENCE

CEMETERY OF SAINT PIERRE
Paul Cezanne (1839-1906) Artist

PROVENCE-ALPES-COTE D'AZUR

CASTLE VAUVENARGUES ESTATE GROUNDS (Private)
Pablo Piccasso (1881-1973) Artist

CHAMPAGNE-ARDENNE

COLOMBEY-Les-DEUX-EGLISES PARISH CHURCHYARD
General Charles de Gaulle (1890-1970) French President

ESSOYES, CHAMPAGNE - ARDENNE

ESSOYES CEMETERY
Auguste Renoir (1841-1919) Impressionist Painter, Sculptor

GIVERNY

GIVERNY CHURCH CEMETERY
Claude Monet (1840-1926) Impressionist Painter

PARIS

DE PASSY CEMETERY
Claude Debussy (1862-1918) Classical Composer
Edouard Manet (1832-1883) Artist
Marcel Renault (1872-1903) Founder of Renault cars with brother Louis

LES INVALIDES
Napoleon Bonaparte (1769-1821) French Emperor

MONTMARTRE CEMETERY
Adolphe Adam (1803-1856) Classical Composer
Andre Ampere (1775-1836) Scientist
Hector Berlioz (1803-1869) Classical Composer
Edward Degas (1834-1917) Artist
Leo Delibes (1836-1891) Classical Composer
Alexandre Dumas (1824-1895) Author
Gustave Moreau (1826 –1898) Artist

Vaslav Nijinsky (1889-1950) Ballet Dancer
Jacques Offenbach (1819-1890) Classical Composer
Adolphe Sax (1814-1894) Musical Instrument Designer
Emile Zola (1840-1902) Novelist (original burial site)

PANTHEON
Louis Braille (1809-1852) Educator, Inventor
Marie Curie (1867-1934) Scientist
Alexandre Dumas (1802-1870) Author
Victor Hugo (1802-1885) Author
Jean-Jacques Rousseau (1712-1778) Philosopher
Voltaire (1694-1778) Philosopher
Emile Zola (1840-1902) Author

PERE LACHAISE CEMETERY
Daniel Francois Esprit Auber (1782-1871) Classical Composer
Georges Bizet (1838-1875) Classical Composer
Maria Callas (1923-1977) Opera Singer
Frederick Francois Chopin (1810-1849) Classical Composer
Eugene Delacroix (1798-1863) Painter
Paul Dukas (1865-1935) Classical Composer
Stephane Grappelli 1908-1997) Jazz Violinist (ashes)
Rene Lalique (1860-1945) Glassmaker
Marcel Marceau (1923-2007) Mime Artist
Yves Montand (1921-1991) Actor
Jim Morrison (1943-1971) Singer "The Doors"
Edith Giovanna Piaff (1915-1963) Singer and Entertainer
Camille Pissarro (1830-1903) Artist
Gioacchino Antonio Rossini (1792-1868) Classical Composer
Georges-Pierre Seurat (1859-1891) Artist
Oscar Wilde (1854-1900) Author and Playwright

SAINT DENIS BASILIQUE
Louis XIV (1638-1715) French King
Louis XVI (1754-1793) French King
Marie Antoinette (1755-1793) French Monarch

SAINTE-GENEVIEVE-DES-BOIS PARIS
RUSSIAN CEMETERY
Rudolph Nureyev (1938-1993) Ballet dancer

LA TOURRAINE

ST ROBERT CHURCHYARD
Yul Brynner (1920-1985) Actor

GERMANY

BERLIN

BERLIN-SCHONEBERG (FRIEDHOF SCHONEBERG III), FRIEDENAU
Marlene Dietrich (1901-1992) Actress, Singer

KREUZBERG DREIFALTKEITSFRIEDHOF FRIEDRICHSHAN –KREUZ
Felix Mendelssohn (1809-1847) Composer

ISLES OF SCILLY

ST MARY'S

ST MARY'S OLD CHURCH CHURCHYARD
Harold Wilson (1916-1995) Prime Minister

ITALY

CAPRI

PROTESTANT CEMETERY
Gracie Fields (1899-1979) Singer, Actress

FLORENCE

BASILICA DI SANTA CROCE
Galilei, Galileo (1564-1642) Scientist
Machiavelli, Niccolo (1469-1527) Political Philosopher
Marconi, Guglielmo (1874-1957) Inventor
Michelangelo (1475-1564) Sculptor, Painter
Rossini, Gioacchino (1792-1868) Classical Composer

ISCHIA

William Walton (1902-1983) Classical Composer

MONTALE EMILIA-ROMAGNA

MONTALE RANGONE CEMETERY
Luciano Pavarotti (1935-2007) Opera singer

MILAN

CIMITERO MONUMENTALE
Arturo Toscanini (1867-1957) Classical Conductor

CASA DI RIPOSO PER MUSICISTI
Giuseppe Verdi (1813-1901)

NAPLES

CIMITERO DI SANTA MARIA DEL PIANTO
Enrico Caruso (1873-1921) Opera singer

PARMA

CEMETERY DELLA VILLETTA
Nicolo Paganini (1782-1840) Violinist

ROME

RECANATI CEMETERY
Beniamino Gigli (1890-1957) Opera singer

TORRE DEL LAGO (Viareggio)

PUCCINI ESTATE GROUNDS
Giacomo Puccini (1858-1924)

VENICE

CEMETERY OF SAN MICHELE
Igor Stravinsky (1882-1971) Classical Composer

JAMAICA

FIREFLY ESTATE, FIREFLY HILL, MONTEGO BAY
Noel Coward (1899-1973) Playwright

MONACO

CATHEDRAL OF ST. NICHOLAS
Grace Kelly (1929-1982) Actress, Princess of Monaco
Prince Louis Ranier (1923-2005) Grimaldi Family Vault

CIMETIERE DE MONACO
Josephine Baker (1906-1975) Singer
Anthony Burgess (1917-1993) Author
Roger Moore (1927-2017) Actor

PANAMA

PANAMA CITY

INGLESA SANTUARIO NATIONAL CEMETERY
Margot Fonteyn (1919-1991) Ballet Dancer

RUSSIA

MOSCOW

KREMLIN WALL
Yuri Andropov (1914-1984) Premier
Leonid Ilyich Brezhnev (1906-1982) General Sec. Communist Party
Yuri Gagarin (1934-1968) Cosmonaut
Josef Stalin (1878-1953) Soviet Leader

RED SQUARE
Vladimir Lenin (1870-1924) Soviet Leader

NOVODEVICHY CEMETERY
Anton Chekhov (1860-1904) Author
Nikita Khrushchev (1894-1971) Soviet Statesman
Sergie Prokofiev (1891-1953) Classical Composer
Mstislav Rostropovich (1927-2007) Cellist
Dmitri Shostakovich (1906-1975) Classical Composer
PEREDELKINO CEMETERY
Boris Pasternak (1890-1960) Author

TULA OBLAST

YASNAYA POLYANA
Leo Tolstoy (1828-1910) Author

ST PETERSBURG

ALEXANDER NEVSKY MONASTERY
Alexander Borodin (1833-1887) Classical Composer
Mikhail Glinka (1804-1857) Classical Composer
Modest Mussorgsky (1839-1881) Classical Composer
Marius Petipa (1822-1910) Ballet Choreographer
Nikolai Rimsky-Korsakov (1844-1908) Classical Composer
Peter Ilych Tchaikovsky (1840-1893) Classical Composer

ST PETER AND PAUL FORTRESS
Alexander I (1777-1825) Russian Monarch
Catherine II The Great (1729-1796) Russian Monarch
Paul I (1754-1801) Russian Monarch
Peter I The Great (1672-1725) Russian Monarch
Nicholas Alexandrovich Romanov (1868-1918) Russian Czar

SERBIA

BELGRADE

Borodin

Mussorsky

Tchaikovsky

Rimsky Korsokov

Tsar Nicholas II

NIKOLA TESLA MUSEUM
Nikola Tesla (1856-1943) Inventor

SPAIN

BARCELONA

SAGRADA FAMILIA
Antoni Gaudi (1852-1926) Architect

SALVADOR DALI MUSEUM
Salvador Dali (1904-1989) Artist

NIKOLA TESLA MUSEUM
Nikola Tesla (1856-1943) Inventor

MADRID

CHURCH OF SAN JUAN BAUTISTA (Now demolished)
Diego Rodriguez de Silva Velasquez (1599-1660) Artist

SWITZERLAND

CORSIER-SUR-VEVEY

CORSIER CEMETERY
Charlie Chaplin (1889-1977) Comedy Actor

GENEVA

CEMITIERE DES ROIS
Ernest Ansermet (1883-1969) Classical conductor
Humphrey Davy (1779-1829) Chemist, Scientist

CELIGNY, GENEVE CANTON
VIEUX CEMETERY
Richard Burton (1925-1984) Actor
Alistair MacLean (1922-1987) Author "Guns of Navarone"

REFERENCES

English Heritage Blue Plaques

Liverpool Blue Plaques

Find a Grave

The Shady Old Lady's Guide to London

Notable Abodes

Arthur Lloyd

The British Comedy Society

The Heritage Foundation U.K.

Beverley Hills Historical Society

The Movieland Directory

British Plaque Trust

London's Blue Plaques (Howard Spencer)

seeing-stars.com

John's Star Maps